29

41st State to join the Union

SCENE: ST. MARY LAKE,
GLACIER NATIONAL PARK
STATE FLOWER: BITTERROOT
STATE FLAG
FAMOUS PERSON: GRANVILLE STUART

MONTANA

by Dorothy M. Johnson

Huge, beautiful Montana is a state of high mountains, rolling prairies, wheat-fields, ranches, and untold mineral riches. On the slopes of her Rockies west of the Continental Divide rise streams that flow to the Pacific. To the east of North America's backbone are the headwaters of the Missouri, which begin their long journey down to the Mississippi and the Gulf.

Dorothy M. Johnson grew up in northwestern Montana, surrounded by the forested Rockies. Her spirited account of the Indians, trappers, gold miners, settlers, and desperadoes of Montana's past and of the sheepherders, cattlemen, farmers, lumberjacks, and the coal and copper miners of the present day offers a broad, panoramic view of a vast, bountiful land. Key industries—lumbering, mining, ranching, farming—are described in comprehensive and fascinating detail. Montana's magnificent parks, wildlife, and scenery, her buffalo and bear and deer and trout, her flowers, her cloudless skies, and a roster of Montanans (from Calamity Jane to Senator Mike Mansfield) are lovingly recorded, too, for the delight of young readers everywhere.

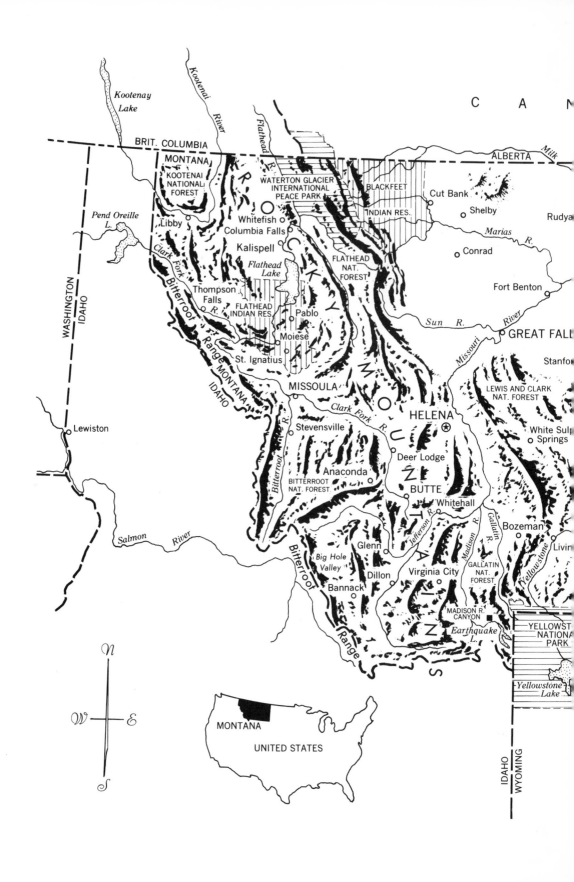

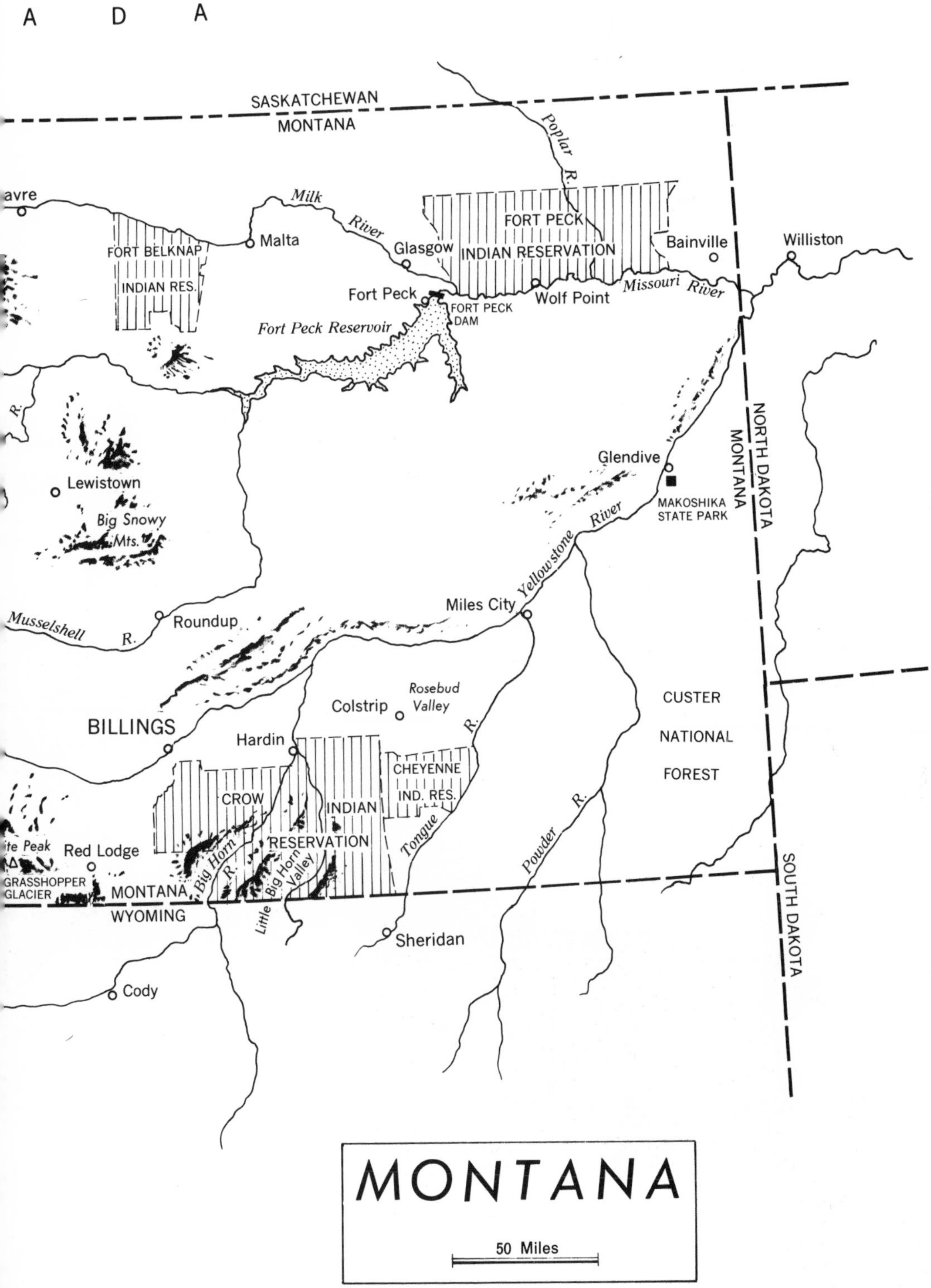

A D A

SASKATCHEWAN
MONTANA

avre

Milk

FORT BELKNAP

Malta

River

Glasgow

Poplar R.

FORT PECK

INDIAN RESERVATION

Bainville

Williston

INDIAN RES.

Fort Peck

FORT PECK
DAM

Wolf Point

Missouri River

Fort Peck Reservoir

R.

Lewistown

Big Snowy
Mts.

Glendive

NORTH DAKOTA
MONTANA

MAKOSHIKA
STATE PARK

Musselshell

R.

Roundup

Yellowstone River

Miles City

BILLINGS

Hardin

Colstrip

Rosebud
Valley

CUSTER

NATIONAL

FOREST

CROW

CHEYENNE
IND. RES.

R.

ite Peak

Red Lodge

INDIAN

RESERVATION

Tongue

Powder R.

GRASSHOPPER
GLACIER

MONTANA

Big Horn R.

Little Big Horn
Valley

WYOMING

Sheridan

SOUTH DAKOTA

Cody

MONTANA

50 Miles

COWARD-McCANN, INC.   **NEW YORK**

Consultant: Mrs. Ruth Longworth
Librarian, Montana State Library

STATES OF THE NATION

MONTANA

by Dorothy M. Johnson

COWARD-McCANN, INC.

PHOTO CREDITS

Montana Chamber of Commerce, pages 21, 34, 49, 50, 86, 89, 96, 107
Montana Historical Society, pages 11, 19, 48, 63, 97, 99, 101, 104
U.S. Department of the Interior: Bureau of Land Management, page 74; Bureau
    of Reclamation, pages 9, 12, 23, 24, 27, 28, 31, 39, 42, 45, 46, 59, 65, 85, 95, 113;
    Bureau of Sport Fisheries & Wildlife, pages 53, 91, 92, 93
U.S. Forest Service, title page; pages 17, 37, 67, 68, 71, 73, 75, 78, 79, 80, 83, 93, 114
Whitney Gallery of Western Art, page 111

Jacket
St. Mary Lake, Glacier National Park: Montana Historical Society
Bitterroot: Montana Highway Commission
State flag: F. E. Compton Co.
Granville Stuart: Montana Historical Society

Maps, Donald T. Pitcher

Title page, Cattle grazing, Beaverhead National Forest

This book about Montana
is dedicated to
Dr. Thora Sorenson, Professor Emerita,
University of Montana

CONTENTS

Chapter 1

A Broad Look at a Big State

Montana, fourth largest of the fifty states, is like two separate worlds. The eastern two-thirds is mostly rolling prairie, the Great Plains. The western third is the big, tumbled Rocky Mountains. They constitute the Continental Divide, so some of our rivers flow east to join the Mississippi, and others flow west to the Columbia. In Glacier National Park there's a mountain called Triple Divide Peak from which streams flow not only east and west but also north to Hudson Bay.

Montana has such great contrasts of rolling prairie and rugged mountains that a person who moves from one end of the state to the other may feel like a homesick foreigner for a while.

I grew up in Whitefish, a railroad town in northwestern Montana, with the forested Rockies all around. I used to admire lumberjacks striding along the streets in hobnailed boots, and lordly locomotive

Sawtooth Mountain

engineers heading for the railroad yards to take trains over "the hump," the Continental Divide.

But we never saw a cowboy except in the movies. East of the Rockies, lucky youngsters not only knew real cowboys but rode their own horses to round up cattle. Some of them, though, must have dreamed about living where there were lots of trees and water deep enough for swimming. *We* had a cold, deep lake seven miles long and could get lost in the forest without going very far from home.

In Whitefish we used to hear tall tales about Paul Bunyan, the mythical lumberjack who was so big that he used a lodgepole pine to brush his teeth. One of these stories explains how Montana happens to be the shape it is on the map:

Montana used to be a rectangle, and so did Idaho. But the year Paul Bunyan logged off eastern Montana, he used a donkey engine to speed up the operation, and he had trouble with that old engine. He worked on it and worked on it until finally it blew up.

The explosion was so powerful that it blew out the western end of Montana and smashed it into northern Idaho. If you don't believe it, just look at the map. Sure enough, the western end of Montana bulges, and Idaho has only a thin panhandle there. And if you don't believe that Paul Bunyan logged off eastern Montana, just try to find any big forests on our prairies. (Every tall tale about Paul Bunyan traditionally ends with "if you don't believe it" and some pretty shaky "proof.")

The giant lumberjack is purely imaginary, but the experiences of some real people, members of the Lewis and Clark Expedition, who explored Montana early in the nineteenth century are almost as hard to believe. Lewis and Clark earned everlasting fame in the history of our nation. They were the leaders of the first exploration party that ever crossed Montana.

The expedition included twenty-nine white men; Clark's Negro servant, York; a Shoshone Indian girl named Sacajawea; her very young baby; and a big dog named Scammon—one of the few dogs that ever made names for themselves in history.

They took part in one of the greatest adventures of all time. President Thomas Jefferson assigned Meriwether Lewis, who was his secretary, and William Clark, an Army officer, to look over the Louisiana Purchase. This was a vast, unknown area that the young United States had just bought, sight unseen, from France. Part of this big real estate purchase later became Montana.

The expedition left St. Louis on May 14, 1804, and returned on September 23, 1806, after traveling about 4,000 miles. More than half those winding miles were in Montana.

Lewis and Clark named rivers and valleys and mountains and landmarks. Think of being the first civilized men to see all this! They found the headwaters of the great Missouri, three rivers that they called the Jefferson, for the President; the Madison, for James Madison, Secretary of State; and the Gallatin, for Albert Gallatin, Secretary of the Treasury.

Lewis named Maria's River (we spell it Marias now) for a cousin, Maria Wood. He was very fond of Maria, but she married somebody else. Clark named the Judith River for a girl he couldn't have known very well at the time, although he married her later. Her nickname was Judy, but her name wasn't Judith, as he supposed; it was Julia Hancock.

Even Sacajawea's baby has a landmark named for him, Pompey's

Mural of Lewis and Clark Expedition, in Capitol Building

Missouri River, near Lewiston

Pillar. His mother called him Pomp. His "pillar" is a great, flat-topped rock in the Yellowstone Valley. You can still see "Wm. Clark, July 25, 1806," where Clark carved it on the rock.

The expedition leaders named the Great Falls of the Missouri, where the city of Great Falls is now. They spent twenty-six days in the hard work of portaging—that is, carrying their boats and baggage —about 18 miles around the Great Falls.

On the east side of the Continental Divide, near the top, the explorers found a spring that they decided was the very beginning of the Missouri River. One of their men, Hugh McNeal, stood with one foot on each side of the stream and exulted, "Thank God, I have lived to bestride the mighty Missouri!" I bestrode the mighty Missouri at the same place, in the Sacajawea Memorial Area, about 150 years later and got my feet wet. McNeal no doubt had longer legs than mine.

The Indians were fascinated by York, the Negro member of the expedition. The red men had seen a few white men, but they had never seen a black man. They flocked around him, admiring and curious. After the expedition ended, York went back to the Indians and became a chief in one of the tribes.

Lewis and Clark had instructions to find out whether there was a Northwest Passage, a water route through the big mountains that were out there. There should be, President Jefferson thought. A boat should be able to go up rivers to the mountains and then, just over the ridge, there should be another river flowing westward to the Pacific Ocean.

But the expedition ran out of navigable rivers in the Rockies and had to buy horses from the Shoshone Indians and plod through a maze of mountains. First they had to catch up with some of the Shoshones, who were scared to death of them. But Sacajawea was a help. She spoke the language, and her brother was chief of the tribe. York was a help, too. The Shoshones were as much interested in him as they were in the presents that the explorers offered in exchange for horses. The explorers almost starved, but they did cross the Rockies and find a river that flowed into the Columbia. Then they built boats and went on to the Pacific Ocean.

Hard on the heels of Lewis and Clark came fur traders and trappers, bold adventurers who became known as the mountain men. What was the potential of the fur trade? There was a tremendous market for beaver pelts, because every well-dressed man in the United States and Europe wore a beaver hat. How much business could traders do with the Western Indians who trapped beaver? A lot of business, it turned out.

In 1807, Manuel Lisa took a crew of men up the Missouri from St. Louis to buy furs from the Indians. He built a trading post where the Big Horn River flows into the Yellowstone. That was the first building in Montana.

In no time, several fur companies were squabbling for furs. They didn't all come from the United States. David Thompson, employed by the North West Company, a British firm, entered Montana by the back door, from the north and west, in 1809 and built a post at Thompson Falls (which is named for him) on the Clark Fork River. The very first recorded celebration of Christmas in Montana took place there. The post was named Saleesh House.

The doughty mountain men, the trappers, didn't contribute anything to Montana except some great true stories of valor and endurance. They didn't intend to stay here—although several of them stayed involuntarily, because they were killed by Indians. One who told a story that nobody believed was John Colter, who came with Lewis and Clark and stayed because he liked the wilderness. Returning from a long, solitary journey, he told of a place where steam spouted up out of the ground.

Other trappers howled with glee at that tall tale. But the place they laughingly called Colter's Hell turned out to be just as he said it was. It is now Yellowstone National Park, and the northern part of it is in Montana.

The fur business declined because of a change in fashion far away. Gentlemen no longer wanted beaver hats. So almost nobody wanted Montana anymore. The only permanent settlement that remained was Fort Benton, a trading post established in 1847 on the Missouri River.

The first travelers who came to build and to stay awhile arrived in 1841. They were the "black robes," missionaries, three Catholic priests and three lay brothers. Their leader was Father Pierre Jean De Smet, a Belgian. In the beautiful Bitterroot Valley, where the Flathead Indians lived, they constructed the first church building in Montana, of logs. That one is gone now, but another, St. Mary's Mission, was built twenty-odd years later, and you can still see it at Stevensville, with a new church beside it and jagged mountain peaks behind.

The same Jesuit missionaries founded a mission at St. Ignatius, in the Mission Valley, in 1854. One log cabin that is still there is the oldest building remaining in Montana.

All this time, what is now Montana had no attraction at all for ordinary people, the kind who live in houses and raise families and vote and complain about taxes. They found plenty of other places to live. From the East many of them went West with their families in covered wagons, to California or the Oregon country. They didn't even go through Montana. They went to the south, through Wyoming, along the Oregon Trail. Montana was unpopular. Our eastern plains were just part of the Great American Desert, which nobody thought would ever support farming, and our western mountains were simply an obstacle.

. . . Until in 1862 some wandering prospectors found gold in a stream they named Grasshopper Creek—and suddenly thousands of people found a good reason for moving in. Think of it—for half a century nobody wanted Montana except trappers, a few dedicated missionaries, and roving Indian tribes. Gold made all the difference.

Resources Map

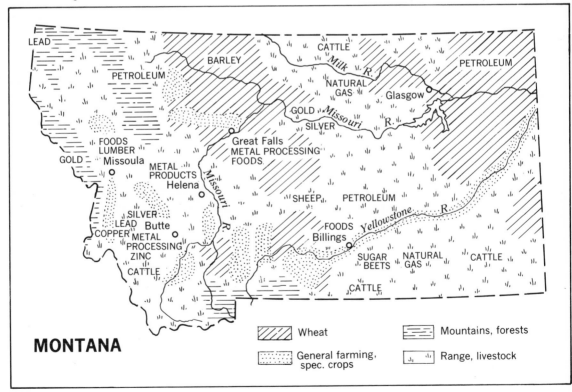

Is it any wonder that we call Montana the Treasure State? The treasure in the earth brought people here.

In Montana now, more than 2,000,000 beef cattle and 1,500,000 sheep fatten on the grass where wild buffalo used to roam. Endless tons of grain, hay and sugar beets are harvested every year from land that didn't look good to farmers. Vast quantities of lumber come from the mountains that were once just in the way. We're still rich in mineral wealth. But it took fifty years for people to begin to find out what Montana was good for, and then they had to learn to live with the climate.

You never see a report in the newspapers that we're having fine weather in Montana. That doesn't make news. What you hear about are our extremes of cold weather or hot weather. Some crops won't grow in Montana because of the climate—but others grow marvelously well for the same reason.

We'd appreciate getting more rain and snow in areas on the prairie where the average annual precipitation is a skimpy 10, 12, or 14 inches, but we've learned to use what we get. We have learned to use the heavy snowfall in our mountains, too. Instead of complaining about it, we ski on it. On the high mountains, snowfall may add up to several hundred inches in one winter. Spring always comes, the snow melts, and we use the water for irrigation, power, and some of our towns' water supplies.

East of the Rockies we sometimes have in January or February a remarkable warm wind called a chinook. The chinook shoots the temperature up in a few hours, and you can actually watch the snow melt.

Outdoor Montana is not gaudy. We have no forests of deciduous trees. We have gentle colors—aspen groves are pale yellow in the spring, and some brush is rose-colored. Sagebrush—we have miles and miles of it—is gray-green.

Most of our big conifers stay dark green, with no giddy nonsense of changing color and then losing all their clothes. A fir or a pine or a spruce stays green and keeps its dignity.

Larch, also called tamarack, has needles, like the evergreen conifers, but they turn yellow in the fall and drop off. Autumn visitors,

16

seeing great patches of yellow on the mountainsides, sometimes worry that some awful disease has attacked the forests. It's not so. The larch is supposed to turn yellow.

The prairie is carpeted with wild flowers in the spring. In the mountains, the spectacular bear grass blooms in early summer. Great clumps of white flowers stand three feet high among the trees. They look like big lighted candles all ready to be carried in a religious procession.

Our state flower is the bitterroot, rose-pink and very pretty, but you can spend a lifetime in Montana without ever seeing one. It likes dry hillsides and it stays in sight only about six weeks a year. The forked white root used to be a staple food of some Indian tribes, who put it in stews and sauces. Once I went with some Flathead Indians to dig it in the spring, when the leaves were tiny and the buds not yet in sight. I stooped and peered at the ground and dug a total of five skinny little roots in half a day. Joe Bigsam laughed and said, "Dorothy, if you had to live on that stuff, you'd starve."

Bear grass in bloom

Chapter 2

Treasure in the Earth

Gold

When prospectors flocked to the diggings on Grasshopper Creek, the town of Bannack grew there. The gold they found was placer gold. A man with a shovel could dig it right out of the ground, along with dirt and gravel that he washed away with water.

Placer mining was a poor man's dream. It didn't require any big investment of capital, as hard-rock mining does. All a man needed was a strong back. One mining claim at Bannack was sold by its discoverer for $600. In two days, four men took $950 in gold from it, using crude equipment that they made themselves.

During the first year of activity at the Grasshopper diggings at Bannack, beginning with the discovery on July 28, 1862, the mines produced $5,000,000 in dust—nuggets and fine bits of the precious metal.

Gold discoveries began the settlement of neglected Montana. A

Panning for gold, circa 1862

group of roving adventurers made a rich strike at Alder Gulch on May 26, 1863, and swarms of miners deserted the earlier strike to go over there. Twelve camps grew up along the stream. The most important one—and the only one that developed into a permanent town—was Virginia City. In five years, Alder Gulch produced between $30,000,000 and $40,000,000 in gold.

In July, 1864, four men who had been prospecting in the Prickly Pear Valley decided to give up, but they went back for one more attempt. They struck it rich and named the place Last Chance Gulch. Later that year the miners who had flocked in changed the name to Helena. The town that grew up there is now the capital of Montana, and its winding main street is Last Chance Gulch.

In December, 1864, 35 miles east of Helena, there was another discovery. This was called Confederate Gulch. There's no town there now. Legend says that in the summer of 1866 three men took out of one small plot of ground 2,100 *pounds* of gold.

Before the gold rush, the whole of Montana had only a few hundred non-Indian inhabitants. Within a year or so, it had 15,000. Gold brought people, and the people brought a need for government. The men who swarmed into the diggings set up a simple, crude kind of government, with the protection of their mining claims as its chief object. There had to be rules so that one man could say to other gold-hungry men, "This claim that I have staked off is mine, and you can't dig here. Go find your own."

Many of them had lived in gold camps in California and Idaho, so they set up, by mutual consent, the same system that worked there. They formed a mining district, agreed on rules about the size of claims, and elected officers: a president, a recorder, a judge to settle disputes (there were plenty of disputes), and a sheriff to enforce the settlements.

A smooth-talking, fast-shooting man named Henry Plummer got into a quarrel with the first sheriff, Henry Crawford, who shot him in the arm. Then Crawford prudently left Montana forever, and Plummer was elected sheriff.

Plummer was a villain with a lurid past and a very brief future. He had left a trail of dead men behind him in the mining camps of

20

Capitol Building, Helena

California and Idaho, but this fact didn't come to light until later. Plummer was head of a gang of about fifty murderers and holdup men who called themselves the Innocents. Other people called them road agents, but in whispers. Sheriff Plummer's deputies were villains, too, all but one. The others arrogantly shot that one down in public and went unpunished for their crime.

More than a hundred men were killed or simply disappeared before the decent men of the Montana gold camps realized that the road agents were organized. After a particularly brutal killing, just before Christmas, 1863, a group of angry businessmen and miners rounded up several suspects, held a public trial, and hanged one of the guilty men, George Ives.

Then two dozen solid citizens who knew they could trust one another held a very secret meeting and organized a committee of vigilance. This was an institution—sometimes good, sometimes bad, always potentially dangerous—that had sprung up in lawless communities in the West.

Vigilance committees had no sanction under the law. They came

21

into existence in emergency situations, when desperate measures were required. San Francisco had vigilantes in the gold rush days of '49.

The Montana vigilantes rode far and fast, tracking down road agents. They never held public trials of the men they suspected—and this in itself is dangerous, because every accused person is entitled to a public trial. But they did bring order, if not peace, to the sprawling communities in the goldfields. In six weeks, they captured, tried, and executed twenty-six of the road agents—including Sheriff Henry Plummer.

He and two of his deputies were hanged on January 10, 1864, in Bannack. In Virginia City, in an empty old building, you can still see the beam from which five other villains dangled four days later. On a barren hill above the town you can look at their graves, each marked with a man's name, the date, and the word "hanged." That's a spooky place, especially when you recall that eight more road agents are buried there in unmarked graves—an unlucky thirteen of very bad men.

We have a mystery in our history: 3–7–77. The vigilantes used those numbers to warn outlaws that they had a quick choice to make: Get out or get hanged. The mysterious numbers were used by vigilante groups in Bannack, Virginia City, and Helena during the gold rush.

But nobody knows why those particular numbers were used. Some people say they signified the dimensions of a grave: 3 feet wide, 7 feet long, 77 inches deep. Or maybe they meant that the bad man had 3 hours, 7 minutes, and 77 seconds to pack up, saddle his horse, and get out of there. Whatever the meaning was, the warning was usually effective. But if the vigilantes knew that an outlaw was guilty of murder, they didn't bother to warn him with numbers. They just got a rope and strung him up on a tree or a corral gate.

Government in Montana began with the grim work of the vigilantes. Government is protection, and the peaceable people in the gold camps had no protection until the vigilantes organized. In our state, to be descended from a vigilante is something to boast about.

Montana got its present boundaries and its name when Congress made it a separate territory in 1864. Then it had its own legal gov-

Nevada City, ghost town

ernment, with its first capital in Bannack. Montana Territory was formed to provide the protection of government where the people were. They needed mining laws, roads, schools, tax money, and judges to decide disputes about such matters as property ownership. When western Montana was part of Idaho Territory, the people of Virginia City, for example, had to travel 600 miles to the territorial capital and couldn't get there at all in the winter.

Copper

Gold mining is of no importance in Montana now, but the search for it uncovered ores bearing another metal: copper. This discovery had a tremendous and lasting effect on our economy, for copper mining became one of our big industries. The Anaconda Company, which owns all the mines in Butte, is the state's biggest employer and biggest taxpayer.

Butte is a startling and fabulous city. It grew from a little community that almost died when the gold there played out. One man stuck it out and scraped together enough capital to mine silver, but there was a lot of copper in the ore, and it was a great nuisance.

Hardly anybody wanted copper until the electrical industry came along. Copper and electricity grew up together. The electrical industry uses fully half the copper produced now. The telephone, invented in 1876, also created a big demand for copper. And there it was, and there it is, in the Boulder Batholith, 70 miles long, 35 miles wide, and nobody knows how deep.

A batholith is a mass of igneous rock that was once so hot that it was fluid. It shoved up from deep in the earth's interior. The big rock of the Boulder Batholith is called granite—except by mining specialists, who identify it as quartz monzonite. The central core is copper, with zinc, lead, and other minerals around it.

Butte calls itself "the richest hill on earth," and it is. Seventeen *billion* pounds of finished copper have come out of ore from that hill, and geologists know there's even more copper ore still in the ground.

Butte prides itself on being a mile high and a mile deep. It is, with some to spare. The collar of the Mountain Con mine shaft, Butte's deepest, is 6,135 feet above sea level, and the mine, more than a mile deep, is going still deeper.

Berkeley Pit, an open copper mine, encroaches on the city of Butte.

Several tall, angular structures loom against the sky above the hilly city. They are headframes supporting cables and machinery to move things up and down. These headframes startle tourists, who wonder whether they're gallows for hanging desperadoes.

There's a busy life underground in Butte. The minerals are concentrated in veins, and miners follow them vertically, horizontally, or on a slant. There are tracks and trains down there, water pipes, communication lines, and pipes to carry compressed air, which provides power for drilling into the rock. Fresh air goes down there, too—11 tons of it for each ton of rock hoisted out.

Where several old mine shafts and some of the city's houses used to be, there is now a whopping big hole in the ground, so vast that you have to look twice to see all the way across it—7,100 feet from east to west. This is the Berkeley Pit, opened in 1955. Here is open-pit mining, not underground but with everything in plain sight. Huge machines move ponderously around on big terraces like stair steps, gnawing mouthfuls of dirt that is really low-grade copper ore.

The pit uses almost 250 vehicles, including 95 ore-hauling units with a capacity from 65 to 100 tons. The big shovels can load a 100-ton truck in three bites, taking about two minutes.

Even the holes bored for blasting the rock are big—9 inches across and 40 feet deep.

Although open-pit mining is hugely expensive, it is cheaper than underground mining, which requires air-conditioning and ventilating machinery. But underground mining produces high-grade ore, as much as 60 pounds of copper to a ton, with a little silver and gold. Pit ore produces about 15 pounds of copper to the ton. More men still work underground in the Butte mines than in the open pit.

Chemistry on a big scale removes the metal from the ore—which looks like ordinary dirt to a nonminer. A lot of water is involved in this process. Water pumped from underground has some copper in it; sulfuric acid is added, and this water leaches copper out of the great piles of very low-grade ore.

Part of the chemistry requires pumping the material to the "tin can mine," an idea that amuses everybody. This is the precipitation plant, and it's full of old tin cans, collected from dumps and shredded. The water circulates over the tin cans, and through a chemical process copper replaces the iron in them. The tin cans become sludge with a high copper content. It goes to a smelter at Anaconda, 26 miles away, by railroad. High-grade ore from the deep mines is smelted in Anaconda, too.

The world price of copper is important in Butte, and it fluctuates. Cost is the most important factor in deciding what mining method to use. A man working underground may produce 11 to 20 tons of high-grade ore in a day, while a man on the surface, in the Berkeley Pit, produces from 60 to 200 tons of low-grade ore. The deeper a mine goes, the more expensive it is to bring up the ore. When the world price of copper goes up only two cents a pound, that may be enough to make it worth while to stress deep (vein) mining.

Pit mining produces the most ore at the lowest cost. The rock averages 15 pounds of copper per ton—about $6 worth when copper sells for 40 cents. This doesn't seem like much money for digging out and processing a ton of anything, especially when you realize that for every ton of rock they take out, they have to move four tons or more of material that has little value, if any.

The Anaconda Company follows a plan of ton-for-ton ore reserve. That is, for each ton of copper ore they mine at 4,800 feet, for example, experts are doing exploration work to find another ton 100 feet deeper. "Exploration" doesn't mean that a geologist is hacking away down there with a pick. He does most of his work up above— sometimes far above, in an airplane. He uses aerial photographs, aerial magnetic surveys, and soil sampling, among other tools. Infrared photographs show him, from changes in the composition of vegetation and soil on the surface, that minerals are present under the ground.

Manufacturing

One of the treasures of the Treasure State is waterpower. There is a lot of waterpower at the Great Falls of the Missouri River. The city of Great Falls is, therefore, a busy manufacturing center. Copper is refined there by an electrolytic process. Then it is melted in fur-

Yellowtail Dam, at Bighorn Canyon

naces and cast into molds to be shipped to fabricating plants.

The Anaconda Wire and Cable Company at Great Falls fabricates both copper and aluminum products. This company also has plants in nine other states.

Columbia Falls, in western Montana, is a little town that used to be quiet. It boomed to prosperity after the Hungry Horse Dam was built a few miles away on the South Fork of the Flathead River. The Anaconda Aluminum Company chose Columbia Falls as the site for a big aluminum plant because land, workers, and cheap electric power were available there. Hundreds of people work in the aluminum plant now.

The raw material used at the plant travels great distances. An ore called bauxite goes by ship from Jamaica in the West Indies to New Orleans, where it is refined to make alumina. Two pounds of bauxite make one pound of alumina.

From New Orleans the alumina travels to western Montana by railroad, and at Columbia Falls it becomes aluminum. Two pounds of alumina make one pound of aluminum.

27

Industrial plants, Billings

Another way to get the raw material to the Montana factory is planned: Alumina will be refined in Jamaica and then moved by ship clear around to the west coast of the United States, to the port of Everett, Washington, and then to Columbia Falls by railroad.

The plant has five potlines. Each is a series of pots, and a pot is really an electric furnace. This plant has 120 pots to a line, and each pot can produce more than 1,500 pounds of aluminum every twenty-four hours.

The hot, liquid aluminum is cast into ingots that sometimes weigh as much as eight tons each. They travel on specially designed railway flatcars to other factories for further processing.

Manufacturing is not yet an activity that comes to mind when you think about Montana, but it is going to increase as more people recognize one of our attractions: We have plenty of room. Some people who live in crowded areas have to travel for two hours before they can start to earn a living. We have no crowded areas. We drive to work in a few minutes and have more hours to spend as we wish.

Land for factories is becoming scarce and high-priced in many states. We have land in abundance, and it is not high-priced because our population is small. If all the people in Montana spread out evenly, there would be only four and a fraction of us in each square mile. Each of fourteen cities in the United States has more people in it than the whole state of Montana. Twenty-two of our fifty-six counties have fewer than 5,000 inhabitants in each.

Our people are an even more important resource than our land. A friend of mine remarked, "Kids who grow up on ranches are fine workers. They're used to putting in eight hours of work for eight hours of pay. And they're self-reliant. If a boy on a farm can't find a part to repair a machine, he'll make one. The Indians on our seven reservations develop into self-reliant workers, too, and they have complete control of their emotions. They don't fly apart under stress."

Coal

Way back in 1876 a Chicago newspaperman named John F. Finerty was mighty impressed by the coal he saw in southern Montana. Lumps of it stuck out of canyon walls, and the ground was black with its dust. He saw two coal ledges burning. The whole valley of the Rosebud, he concluded, was a huge coal bed.

Finerty wasn't looking for coal. He was a front-line war correspondent with General George Crook, who was chasing Sioux Indians. Crook's command found them and fought them at the Battle of the Rosebud, but he didn't defeat them. A couple of weeks later, Lieutenant Colonel George Armstrong Custer found them in the Little Big Horn Valley, and they defeated *him*. A New York newspaperman with Custer was among those killed.

Finerty was lucky. He lived to write a book about his frontier experiences, *War-Path and Bivouac*. He was a good reporter, and he noticed everything. He wrote about Montana's coal, "Some day, I thought, when the Sioux are all in the happy hunting grounds, this valley will rival the Lehigh of Pennsylvania."

But Montana's Rosebud has never rivaled Pennsylvania's Lehigh in coal production. Montana is not famous for coal mining. Most people, even in Montana, are astonished when they're told that we have more bituminous reserves—estimated at 222 billion tons—than any other state except one.

Which one is unknown. It may be North Dakota; it may be Utah; next week it may be some other state. Or Montana may turn out to be first instead of second. Statistics on coal reserves can't be pinned down; they keep changing. Geologists haven't found all the reserves yet, and as they discover more, the figures change.

There has been some coal mining in Montana for years. In 1918 about 1,600 coal miners were working in the mines near Red Lodge. In 1967 the last big mine closed. The coal there and near Roundup, which used to have busy coal mines, is far underground and expensive to get out. Natural gas, some of it piped in from Canada, is now preferred as a fuel. A few "wagon mines" remain, from which farmers haul coal for their own use.

Montana's coal is part of the Fort Union formation, probably the largest coal basin on earth. It extends under parts of Wyoming, North Dakota, and Saskatchewan.

We still have most of the coal we started with. Ninety percent of it lies under the eastern third of the state. An important new use for it has been developed: to make steam to produce electric power. That idea would startle Finerty, because when he was reporting on Indians in 1876, Thomas Alva Edison and a few other dreamers back East were just beginning to work out some theories about electricity, and nobody in the world had electric lights.

Montana-Dakota Utilities has been using eastern Montana lignite in a plant at Sidney since 1958 to produce power. In 1968 Montana Power Company began producing power from bituminous coal in a new plant in Billings. This coal comes from the very same part of the state that impressed Finerty, the Rosebud Valley. Montana Power bought a whole town there, named Colstrip. It has paved streets, houses, a store, and a school with a gymnasium and theater.

Colstrip was developed by the Northern Pacific Railway, which mined some 40,000,000 tons and used to burn coal in all its locomotives between Minneapolis and Idaho. But when the NP converted from coal-burning locomotives to diesels, the railroad didn't need any more coal.

Power companies, however, have an increasing need for sources of power in addition to waterpower. Montana Power Company will need four times as much electric power in the year 2000 as it did when its coal steam plant was built in Billings. The company has leases on a comfortable 850,000,000 tons of coal, more than it's going to need for a long, long time.

Colstrip's coal moves to Billings, about 100 miles away, at the rate of two or three trainloads a week, and in a few years a trainload a day will be needed there. Great quantities are also shipped to power plants in other states.

The Billings steam plant has a stack 350 feet high through which the smoke is discharged to minimize air pollution. Electrostatic precipitators remove the ash from the gas as it goes up through the stack, and the resulting dust is collected and stored. Even the dust is used, as a filler in asphalt for building highways.

The future of Montana's coal is more exciting than its past. Sometime coal will be liquefied to make synthetic crude oil, from which gasoline can be refined. And there's a potential market for our coal in Oregon, where steel mills now bring it all the way from West Virginia.

Strip mining for coal, Colstrip

The Rosebud Valley's bituminous coal is remarkably free from impurities, and it's easy to get out by stripping. That is, the overburden—the earth and rock on top of it—is loosened by blasting, and then the coal is loaded onto trains with huge mechanical shovels.

Underground mining is expensive. You can take out only about half the coal, because you have to leave columns of it to hold up the roof. One man working one day may be able to take out 13 tons.

But stripping can produce 100 tons per man-day, and there's nothing to cave in, so about 95 percent of the coal can be taken out.

Like several other states, Montana has a law providing for the reclamation of strip-coal-mined lands. The company that does the mining, the landowner (public or private), and the Montana Bureau of Mines and Geology determine how the stripped country will be reclaimed and how it will be used: for forest, range for stock, growing crops, recreation, or industry.

Land that is reclaimed after stripping is actually improved. It is no longer monotonously flat and barren-looking. With the rocks loosened, rain filters into the ground so that plants can grow. Colstrip has, in fact, a fine recreation area—developed from an old mine pit—that attracts visitors for camping, swimming, fishing, and picnics.

Specialities from the Earth

Two substances that come from the earth are of increasing economic importance in Montana, although most people have never heard of them. They are bentonite and vermiculite.

Bentonite—called the clay with a hundred uses—is produced in quantity near Glasgow. Bentonite is a bonding agent; that is, it holds things together. It swells greatly in contact with water. The oil industry needs it for drilling wells, and the steel industry uses it to pelletize taconite.

What does that mean in plain English? Taconite is granite rock with a little iron ore in it. A lot of taconite is mined in northern Minnesota. It is ground up and the iron ore, separated from the rock by a magnetic process, mixed with bentonite and made into

32

pellets for easy handling in transportation to steel plants. When taconite is in pellets, the iron can be more easily extracted in blast furnaces.

In a new $2,000,000 plant near Glasgow, bentonite is thoroughly dried and pulverized. At peak production, the mill can ship eighteen carloads a day. A division of the Ashland Oil and Refining Company strip mines the mineral on about 16,000 acres. There are two big fields of bentonite there, each about 30 miles long.

Near Libby, in the far northwestern corner of Montana, is the biggest vermiculite mine in the United States. Vermiculite is a mineral that expands greatly when heated, so that it fills up spaces but weighs very little. It is used for insulation, for soundproofing, and for padding in packages.

Oil

The oil industry employs specialists in various sciences such as geology, chemistry, paleontology, and physics. Some of these people blithely use words like *paleozoic, stratigraphic trap, lacustrine, paludal, thribble, fourble, anticline, geosyncline, basement complex,* and *isomerization.* Not all of them talk this way all the time, however. They also say, "My wife told me to bring home a dozen eggs," or, "It's going to be hot again today," like anybody else.

A couple of terms that should be explained (other than the peculiar ones just mentioned) are *wildcat* and *dry hole.* Anybody in Montana's oil and gas areas (which include thirty-one of our fifty-six counties) understands these.

A wildcat is an oil well drilled in territory where oil hasn't been found before. It's a gamble, because an oil well doesn't necessarily produce oil, although the people who drilled it had scientific reasons for hoping that it would. Before you invest $50,000 or more in drilling a hole in the ground, you want to have some sound basis for the decision.

But the sad fact is that only about one out of every ten wildcats does strike oil, and the odds against finding oil that can be developed profitably are 100 to 3. Finding oil is one thing; finding

33

Oil rig, near Billings

enough oil, which can be worked commercially and transported economically to a refinery, is something else again.

A dry hole is a well that didn't work out. It's not necessarily dry. Water, gas, or even some oil may be there, but not in commercial quantities. A dry hole may also be called a duster.

Oil doesn't come in pools underground, although artists' drawings of oil wells make it look that way. Actually, it is mixed with sand, or it is even in rock. Oil shale looks like rock as solid as any, but there's oil in it. *Petroleum* comes from the Latin words for rock and oil; it really is "rock oil."

Billings is the center of the oil industry in Montana, although there are no oilfields near that city. But because of excellent railroad and truck transportation facilities, Billings became a refining center. Most oil and oil products now travel three feet underground through eight-inch pipelines, pushed along by pressure. Some petroleum products go all the way from Billings to Spokane, Washington, and Minot, North Dakota, by pipeline—more than 500 miles east or west.

It's not safe to quote statistics on Montana's petroleum production or on much of anything else about petroleum anywhere, because something new may change the picture half an hour from now. But it is safe to say that Montana east of the Rockies has several oilfields and many oil wells, and that among the thirty-one states that produce oil we're in about twelfth place.

Chapter 3

Treasure on the Earth

Cattle

Movies and television may give the impression that cowboys have as their major objective the rescuing of fair maidens and the shooting of bad guys. That's fiction. In real life, the cattle business is and always was a *business*. Stockmen raise cattle in order to sell them, and they hire cowboys to help produce good beef and get it to market.

Montana still has cowboys, but a man who is dressed like a cowboy may be a real estate salesman or a grocer or a fry cook in a café. We just like Western clothes.

Cowboys still ride horses when they work with cattle. It's not convenient to maneuver around in a Jeep or rope a steer from the back of a truck. Sometimes you'll even see a saddle horse hitched to a parking meter. Once in Miles City I saw a cowboy walking down the street with his horse following him. He wasn't leading it. I suppose it just didn't want to lose him.

Cowboys herding black Angus cattle

But cowboys spend more time riding tractors than riding horses, and they seldom carry six-guns. They shoot only when an injured animal has to be put out of its misery.

The first big market for beef in Montana consisted of the men who dug for gold. They produced nothing *but* gold. They needed food, especially meat, and it didn't have to be tender. They didn't have time to go chasing buffalo herds. There was the market for beef, a sudden market of several thousand hungry men. And a few pioneers saw that mining gold wasn't the only way to become prosperous.

A young man from Denmark, Conrad Kohrs, started our first cattle empire. He went to Bannack looking for gold but got a job as a butcher. Eventually he took over the business, took on a partner, and had more demand for meat than he could supply.

Far to the south, across Wyoming, wound the Oregon Trail, where westward-moving wagon trains often had to leave oxen behind when their feet got sore and their strength gave out. Kohrs drove them up through the mountains and bought other animals from settlers who came into the gold gulches. He ceased to be a butcher boy and became a cattle king.

Another early cattle king was Nelson Story, who brought the first trail herd to Montana from Texas in spite of hordes of Indians who barred the way. The United States Army barred the way, too, at three forts along the Bozeman Trail, and told Story to turn back, but he and his fighting cowboys took the cattle through just the same.

Bringing in cattle to sell immediately as meat was one thing. Ranching was a more permanent undertaking. It took more planning. Montana had miles of grass on which the endless herds of wild buffalo had thrived, and Longhorn cattle thrived on it, too. Legend says that at one time Con Kohrs owned 90,000 head of beef cattle, scattered over the range—free range, open to anybody's herds.

Most Montana beef cattle are Herefords, dark red with white faces—and therefore they are commonly called whitefaces.

They are beef cattle, not dairy cows. Nobody tries to milk a range cow—except her calf. She would be thoroughly indignant, and a Hereford cow that thinks she should protect her calf is much more dangerous than a Hereford bull. These cattle are almost wild. They don't see people very often. Nobody pets them.

Hereford cow with calf

A word of warning: It's not good manners to ask a stockman how many cows he has. That's too much like trying to find out the amount of his bank balance. He will answer courteously but vaguely, "Quite a bunch." If you ask how much land he owns, his reply may be "About as far as you can see." Here are some indications of the size of our cattle ranches:

One stock-growing family in Rosebud County winters about 600 cows every year, owns 30,000 acres, and leases another 50,000. Another family, near Glenn, runs nearly 2,000 head of whitefaces and sells 700 head of yearlings annually. A cow ranch north of Malta includes 48,000 acres, 75 square miles.

Rustling—the stealing of livestock—has always been a problem in Montana. Because of losses to cattle and horse thieves, stockmen organized the Montana Stockgrowers Association, our first trade association. It is still thriving. So is rustling, but ranchers no longer simply hang thieves from the nearest tree.

Stealing a cow or calf (or a horse, sheep, or hog, for that matter) is grand larceny under a Montana law passed in 1894, and the penalty on conviction is from one to fourteen years in the state penitentiary. Many ranchers feel, however, that the courts are too lenient with rustlers. A hunter who shoots an elk out of season is likely to be fined heavily, whereas a cow thief may go free or serve only a light sentence.

Rustlers still operate. A couple of men cut a fence, drive a truck in, load up a bunch of cattle, and get away in the night. But brand inspectors prevent a lot of thievery. Any beef animal that is moved across a county line for legal sale must be checked by an expert who makes sure that the brand on the critter belongs to the man who is selling it. Some ranchers are brand inspectors, and most of our sheriffs are deputy inspectors. They get ten cents a head for checking brands. An inspector has to be able to read any brand and describe it over the telephone so that anybody else in the business can visualize it.

Cattle aren't all that rustlers try to steal. A brand inspector helped two deputy sheriffs collar a thief who was about to rustle a big tractor out of a hayfield.

Present-day stockmen get thoroughly riled about losses to rustlers but don't take the kind of direct action that their fathers used to. There's a story about a rancher near Miles City, forty years ago, who got so mad that he bought a whole case of 30-30 rifles, exactly alike, and gave one to each man in his employ. All he asked was that every man fire one shot every day—he didn't specify the target. Sometime later, a rider came upon a cow that had been butchered—and on the carcass were the bodies of two men. All that could be discovered at the ensuing inquest was that they had been shot with a 30-30 rifle. That stopped the rustling around there.

The early-day cattle business was big business indeed, with the money invested in it coming from men far away, in our Eastern states or the British Isles, who never laid eyes on one of the cows they owned. Everybody seemed to be getting rich, and investors were happy with big dividends, when the bubble broke in the Terrible Winter that made history and changed the whole system of stock raising in Montana. Cattlemen found out that they would have to learn to get along with the climate.

In the spring and summer of 1886, there wasn't enough rain. The grass dried up, and so did streams and water holes—but cattlemen kept on bringing in more herds from Washington and Oregon. The summer was abnormally hot. Vegetation shriveled in the searing wind. Prairie fires roared across the land. The scant water remaining in the shallow streams was so foul with alkali that thirsty horses refused to drink it.

Cattlemen moved some herds to Canada and sold some to the Chicago markets—but the fall rains didn't come, so there were still too many cattle for the meager feed available.

There were signs of a hard winter to come. Wild geese and ducks flew south early, and the cattle grew shaggy coats. Winter came, and it was a hard one, with snowfall drifted by wild blizzards. Cold bit down, and strong young steers froze to death in a bitter storm that lasted for ten days without a letup.

Cattle could survive if they drifted with their backs to the storm, but now parts of the range were fenced with barbed wire. Animals drifted against the fences and died there.

Every stockman and every cowboy was riding, bundled up, suffering in the cold, trying to save the cattle, keeping them back from the rivers, helping them out of drifts. When a thaw came, cold followed it, so that everything was topped by a sheet of ice. One cowboy described it as "hell without the heat."

In March a chinook came, the warm wind that melts snow and ice like magic. The cattlemen rode far to look at their losses. Every coulee was filled with rotting carcasses of cattle that had starved or frozen. Some stockmen lost two-thirds of their herds; some lost 90 percent. Two outfits that started the winter with a total of 27,000 head tallied 250 when it was all over.

To add to the ruin, the bottom dropped out of the price of beef because so many owners had to sell their diminished herds to try to raise money. There were bankruptcies. The dream of the open range ended in a nightmare.

During the decades that have passed since stockmen learned that they must supplement grazing in winter for their animals, haying has become a big operation. In the summer, cattle feed in the high

Feeding Herefords in the winter

places; in winter they are herded down to grass that has been fenced with haystacks not far away.

Some ranches raise hay in irrigated meadows. Irrigation requires the opening up of ditches so the water will flow to the right places. A few ranches provide their irrigators with motorcycles. Alas, the poor cowboy and his faithful horse!

Horses are on the way out for the actual haying job, too. I watched with interest several teams of powerful Belgian workhorses pulling mowers and rakes in a hay meadow. They were wonderfully well trained and nimble with those big feet. But all the men in that hay crew were over sixty years old. The manager of that ranch has since sold his horses and mechanized the whole operation, because it was too hard to get a hay crew.

The fact is that our young men don't know how to handle workhorses, because they grew up with machinery. A young man who can break a green bronc, win prizes in a rodeo, and repair a tractor would probably need half a day to figure out how to harness a team— and then he wouldn't know how to drive.

But haying time is a busy time for Montana boys who want to go back to school with magnificent muscles, an impressive suntan, and money in the bank. Some of them "buck bales"—move and stack them—on a piecework basis. Bucking bales really separates the boys from the men. Three brothers from Missoula did it for several summers while they were in high school. They got a nickel a bale and each of them bucked an average of 460 a day. A bale weighs about 65 pounds, and each bale has to be handled two or three times, so you can figure out for yourself how many tons they lifted.

Baled hay requires special machinery that many ranchers don't have, so they stack loose hay with other specialized equipment— and a summer's work at that makes a man out of a boy, too.

One summer at Bob James' cow ranch on Horse Prairie in Beaverhead County, I was startled to see a big flag flying from the bunkhouse—not the Stars and Stripes but the old Stars and Bars of the Confederate States in the Civil War. The reason is that a couple of his hay hands came all the way from Virginia and brought the rebel flag along for fun. A tradition has grown up among students at the University of Virginia that a fine way to spend the summer is to work for Bob James in Montana.

Down the road a piece, Jack Brenner has had hired help from even farther away. For three summers, he had a student from Oxford University in England. What the Englishman earned didn't pay his plane fare from London (he hitchhiked westward from New York), but he had a fine time and broadened his education.

43

Ranch girls and their mothers sometimes help with the haying if they're not already occupied with cooking grand big meals for the men. A girl who goes back to school in the fall to report, "I drove a buck rake for my dad," has something to boast about.

A buck rake has wooden teeth several feet long—actually, they are thin poles with the ends tapered—and is pushed by a tractor. The driver maneuvers to slide the buck rake under a pile of loose hay that has already been gathered with a tractor-pulled scatter rake; then he whips off toward the big frame where the stack is being built. He pushes the loose hay up onto a sloping apron, also made of poles, and backs away.

This pole apron is called a beaver slide, and you almost have to see it to believe it. A hoist operator on the ground pulls some levers on his machine, a cable grabs, and the enormous beaver slide raises up into the blue sky, folds over, and dumps the hay inside a wooden frame with netting in it to keep the stack in shape.

This is pretty spectacular—and so is the response of the two stackers up on top if the load buries them. This happens when the hoist operator wants to have a little fun. He can see very well what he's doing, and it's no accident when the two men up there, whose job is to spread the hay out evenly, have to dig themselves out from under it.

Nobody ever planted the hay that I watched being stacked. It consists of two dozen or more kinds of wild grasses that were growing there before the first ranchers came. It is harvested year after year, seeds itself, and grows again every year, with no attention other than an annual roughing up of the ground and the application of fertilizer.

Sagebrush grows there, too, and getting rid of it is a problem. In low meadows, you can kill it by flooding it from irrigation ditches. The old way was to dig it up with pick and shovel. The newest way is to hire a helicopter to spray it with chemicals. This works almost like magic. A season later, the big, tough old sagebrush is dead, and among the skeleton bushes the wild grass has zoomed up almost six feet tall. All it wanted was a chance to show what it could do.

The Big Hole Valley in western Montana is the place to see lots

Spring plowing

of hay. The Big Hole is one vast hay meadow with mountains around. It is often called the Valley of Ten Thousand Hay Stacks. Nobody questions that fine, round number, because nobody has patience enough to count.

Techniques are changing. In fact, an industrial revolution is in progress. The machinery for baling or stacking hay will be gone a few years from now, because hay made into pellets has advantages. To make pellets, hay is chopped with machinery, pressed into ropes, then cut into chunks. Hay pellets can be fed to the cattle on a conveyor belt. Pellets are just never going to look as pretty as those tall, neat stacks of loose hay or the building-sized square piles of bales that we're accustomed to admiring.

Like most things connected with ranching, cowboys have changed. They are no longer single men, drifting from one ranch to another,

45

Processing alfalfa for pellets

carrying their soogans and war sacks on horseback and living in
bunkhouses. Most of them are married. Ranchers provide comfortable houses for them and their families. If a cowboy's wife can
cook, they'll both be welcome at good wages on a ranch where the
boss' wife already has her hands full.

Ranch women need to be versatile. Earlier I mentioned Bob
James at Horse Prairie. Both he and his wife, Isabelle, are university
graduates, and both are musicians. Three of their four children are

grown, and the youngest attends country school. For several years Mrs. James was chairman of the school board. Then she ran for the state legislature and was elected. She is an accomplished pianist (her piano tuner comes all the way from San Francisco), a gracious hostess, and a competent bookkeeper and tax accountant for the family business. You can see why she needs a bunkhouse cook to feed the hired hands at hay time and roundup. But if she doesn't happen to have one, she handles that job very well, too. In addition to her other talents, Mrs. James talks to her Shoshone Indian friends in their own language.

One problem common to ranchers and all other families who live far from a town is what to do when the children finish country school and are ready for high school. Thirty or 40 miles or more is just too long a trip to make every day in deep-snow weather. So some high school students board with a family in town, and some attend boarding school far from home in another state. Of course there are some long school bus rides, too.

Just about everyone on a cow ranch who isn't in school turns out to help with the twice-a-year roundups: in the spring to brand the new calves and in the fall to sort out the animals to be shipped and sold. In some parts of Montana, ranchers get together for a cooperative roundup and camp out for several days until the job is finished.

I went on one of these big co-op roundups. Life centered on the mess tent and the chuck wagon, a big truck with all the grub in it and kitchen cupboards built on the back.

The first evening, Oscar the cook brought an ax out of the chuck wagon and neatly slaughtered a long yearling heifer by bashing her over the head. As he knelt to start skinning her, he groaned, "Boys, you made an awful mistake when you roped this one. It's got our own brand on it!"

Everybody laughed, because this idea of expecting to eat stolen beef is an ancient joke, deserving of respect for its antiquity. Besides, good chuck-wagon cooks are scarce, and when one of them makes a joke, *everybody* laughs. The wagon boss, who actually runs the roundup, has more authority, but there is no guarantee that the hired help will think his jokes, if he makes any, are hilarious.

47

Oscar woke everybody up at 2:30 A.M. and cooked a huge breakfast. One of the owners remarked, yawning, "It don't take long to spend the night up here."

We had breakfast in the mess tent and were ready to ride at 4 o'clock, when there was just enough daylight to see the horses' ears.

The men hunted cows and calves out of gullies and off wooded mountains and drove them to a corral to brand the calves. The cowboys' work was dirty and strenuous, but they took a quiet pride in doing it as well as their grandfathers used to—and without as much chance to keep in practice. One man did all the roping in the midst of the bawling, moving, panicky cows and calves in the branding corral. His loop settled exactly every time on the calf he wanted; he could tell which cow owned that calf, and he yelled her brand as his nimble, mind-reading cutting horse dragged the calf to the branding fire.

The men there worked fast, slapping a hot iron on the calf, slitting its ears in the proper earmark to go with that brand, and cutting the little bull calves to make steers of them. It all went so fast that some of the calves didn't even blat, but picked themselves up and ran for their anxious mothers.

Cowboys at the chuck wagon

Outside the corral there were other experts, riders who kept the various bands separate but did not make any mad dashes after strays for fear of getting the whole bunch into a panic.

The cowboys spent the afternoon sleeping in the shade of the mess tent and then stayed up until midnight playing poker. I realized that I would never be able to remember the difference between a straight and a flush, and facing this fact kept me out of the poker game and saved me some money.

One evening somebody brought a bunch of frogs from the creek and we had a frog race. I put a drop of Chanel No. 5 on my entry to encourage him, but this touch of glamor dazzled him so that he wouldn't jump at all.

Sheep

There's an old argument about sheepherders: Does herding sheep drive a man crazy, or does he have to be crazy before he'll herd sheep? This work requires a peculiar temperament. The only kind of man who can stand it is one who likes to be away from the human race for weeks at a time, doing his own cooking in a compact housekeeping sheep wagon, with nobody to talk to except his dog and the sheep.

It's a lonesome job, and few men care for it. But the sheep business has changed in Montana in the past thirty years or so, and few herders are needed, except when flocks feed in the mountains. Most of our sheep now graze in huge fenced pens instead of on the open range. Wire fences prevent them from straying. Thus protected, the sheep don't need the watchful care of a herder.

We used to raise so many sheep that Montana people were all called sheepherders, and we were supposed to be annoyed by this term. We still raise a lot of sheep, but the number has been decreasing every year. Sheep produce two marketable crops: wool that is sheared every year and mutton from the animals when they're slaughtered. Wool is so important a crop that the sheepman's trade organization is the Montana Woolgrowers Association, not the sheep growers.

But many sheepmen have changed over to raising beef cattle. The usual reason for quitting the sheep business is that the market for wool has decreased. Factory-made "miracle fibers," nylon and the long list of others, have replaced wool for many uses. In addition, the importation of finished fabrics from other countries of the world has hurt the market for Montana wool.

Another reason why sheepmen change to cattle is that raising sheep requires a great deal of labor, and men who can be hired to do this skilled work are hard to get.

Even "farm flocks," those that are kept in fenced pens, require care at shearing and at lambing. Cows, on the other hand, don't require much attention. They never have to be sheared. And they're smarter. A whiteface Hereford cow has a blank look and doesn't

Sheepherder

seem very bright, but even a heifer with her first calf identifies it as a marvelous little creature of her very own. She'll look after that baby and fight for it.

A ewe, on the other hand, often has to be persuaded that the little newcomer is really her darling and not an alien visitor from outer space. She'll blat, "What's tha-a-at?" Ewes usually have twin lambs, so the problem is doubled. At lambing time, a flock needs skilled help from human beings, because the ewes become hysterical in all the commotion.

Cows seldom get hysterics. Bob James told me about a time when a bunch of his heifers did lose their wits, though. They were "woofy" —that is, nervous—at being driven into a corral where they would have their first calves. With considerable difficulty, Bob got them

Herding cattle into corral

headed through the gate—and just then there was a sonic boom from a jet that had gone over.

The heifers scattered. Bob's saddle horse bucked like a green bronc. His dog, which was helping herd the animals into the corral, tried to climb up into the saddle with him.

All this happened 45 miles from the nearest town, which just goes to show that you don't have to live near a big metropolitan airport to have civilization catch up with you.

Sheep don't need anything as startling as a sonic boom to bewilder them. You find this out when, driving along a Montana road, you catch up with a flock of sheep. A couple of men on horseback and two or three busy little collies are moving them to a new feed ground or to the shearing pens. The first thing you notice is the choral blatting. Sheep have different voices, but they all repeat the same thing: "Ba-a-ah!"

As soon as they notice your car, they all want to get to the other side of the road. If you stop close behind a car in front of you (by this time, you too are bewildered, caught up in the spirit of the thing), the sheep don't have sense enough to go around. No, they leap over the hood of your car, all complaining about the inconvenience. They make the jump, one after another, more nimbly than you'd think such unathletic creatures were capable of doing.

Sheep lead perilous lives. Among their enemies are eagles, which swoop down and snatch away young lambs. Wild members of the cat family—mountain lions, bobcats, and lynx—are fond of mutton. So are big gray wolves and grizzly bears, but there aren't very many of these animals left.

The worst predators are coyotes, scruffy, sly, sneaky creatures the size of a fairly big dog. Coyotes are fast and smart. They are also prolific. One pair may have as many as seventeen pups in one litter. A coyote will kill a dozen lambs just for the fun of it and eat only one.

Part of a sheepherder's job is to protect his flock from these creatures. A system of predator control has been worked out during the century that sheep have been raised in Montana. Bounties used to be paid for coyote pelts, but some bounty hunters didn't play fair. They killed the pups, all right, but left the adult coyotes to produce more

Coyote   *Black bear*

pups, pelts, and bounties. Finally hunters were hired on straight wages. They weren't tempted to protect coyotes to make sure of a continuing supply.

Montana is divided into four districts for predator control by the Division of Wild Life Services of the U.S. Department of the Interior. Almost thirty men, officially called district field assistants, are now employed year around to shoot, trap, or poison predators.

Coyotes and bears bother both cattle and sheep, especially lambs and calves. When a rancher complains that his stock is being attacked, a troubleshooting district field assistant gets over there as soon as possible and attends to the problem.

Some groups of wool growers also pay bounties for proof that predators have been destroyed.

Some plants are a menace to sheep. Lupine can kill them in late summer when the seedpods are ripe. Death camas is a killer in the spring. Locoweed is the worst plant, though. A sheep that eats loco-weed loses what little wits it had and stands for hours in a stupor, refusing to move to get either food or water.

If a herder has to move a flock across poisonous plants to a new feed ground, he sees to it that the sheep are well filled with good grass so they won't be tempted to commit suicide by eating the bad vegetation.

Sheep have suicidal tendencies anyway. They try to cross streams and can't get out because their wool gets too heavy with water. Sometimes a sheep will try to roll in order to scratch an itch. If it gets squarely on its back and can't turn any farther, it will die inside an hour. For that matter, a horse, a more sensible animal than a sheep, may come to the same sad end, but it takes longer.

Although sheep aren't noted for intellectual achievement, they made a useful discovery countless ages ago. They found that a ewe doesn't have to stay with her own lambs all the time, or take them along when she goes to get a drink of water. So they invented baby-sitting. (So did cows.) One ewe will cuddle down in the shade with a dozen or so lambs while their mothers wander off to enjoy a little freedom.

Like cattle, sheep have to be branded so their owners can identify their property. But whereas cattle are branded with a hot iron, the identifying mark is put on sheep with colored paint that can be scoured off without damage to the wool. Sheep are usually branded right after shearing.

Sheepmen have tried raising all sorts of sheep in Montana, aiming at plentiful lamb production (you can't make money if your ewes have singles instead of twins) and at fleeces that will bring high prices for quality wool. One good thing has to be said for Montana winters: Cold weather makes the sheep grow excellent wool. The Rambouillet breed used to be preferred. Now most of our flocks are Columbias and Targhees.

Unlike several other Western states, Montana has never had any wars between cattle and sheepmen. Cattlemen and cowboys didn't like sheep, which competed with cattle for the free grass on the open range, but they didn't kill solitary herders or drive the helpless animals over cliffs.

The idea of sheep is still distasteful to some old-time stockmen, though. I know a cattleman's wife who likes lamb chops, but the only time she gets them is when she eats in a restaurant in town, and the nearest town is 65 miles from the home ranch. Her husband won't have a sheep on the place, or even a package of its meat in the freezer.

The sheep business lacks romance. We visualize a Biblical shepherd—the boy David, for example, playing a small harp to his snowy-white flock and keeping the wolves off with the slingshot he would later use on Goliath. But a sheepherder is not a shepherd. He's a grown man, with a dog for company and a small radio for music. He needs a shave—who is there to see him?—and instead of a slingshot he has a rifle to use on coyotes. He is a professional at work, guarding a flock of 1,500 or more sheep instead of a dozen.

The cow business has a history of excitement and drama, some of it even true, and the fact that it involves horses keeps the picture rosy. So does the myth that writers have built up about fast-shooting, heroic cowboys. The sheep business, important as it is economically, just hasn't had the right kind of publicity. No writer that I know of ever made a sheepherder seem glamorous. But sheepherders are loyal to their trust. Some of them have been heroes, suffering and dying in blizzards while trying to save their sheep.

The wool growers have dreamed up a publicity idea that involves pretty girls; they're more charming than sheep. This is the annual Miss Wool Contest, sponsored by the American Sheep Producers Council and the Board of City Development of San Angelo, Texas. Sheep-raising states are divided into twenty wool councils, and Montana produces so much wool that it constitutes a council all by itself.

One winner of the national contest was Patti Jo Shaw, a Montana girl, who became Miss Wool for a year. She received a $10,000 wardrobe to be used in fashion shows and television appearances, lived in New York for a year with all expenses paid, and went to Spain for a bit part in a Biblical motion picture, *King of Kings*. In a scene about the Sermon on the Mount, Patti Jo was a shepherdess, leading a small flock of sheep.

After four hours of preparation in a temperature of 110 degrees, 3,000 costumed extras were in place in a valley near Madrid, and it was time to shoot the shepherdess scene. Patti Jo, becomingly draped in a very hot New Testament costume, started down the valley with her sheep. She walked and concentrated and perspired.

The voice of the director, coming over a loudspeaker, shattered the silence: "CUT!" Then he asked scathingly, "Miss Shaw, would you care to see where you have left your flock?"

Patti Jo looked back and found that she had been walking much faster than her sheep. They were the equivalent of three blocks behind her.

That was the end of her movie career, but becoming an actress was not part of her life plan anyway. At the end of her exciting year as Miss Wool, she returned to the University of Montana and earned a degree in journalism.

Another publicity plan attracts girls who can sew. This is the annual Make It Yourself with Wool contest. Girls make and model a coat, a dress, or a two-piece suit of American-manufactured woolen fabric. The grand prize is two weeks in Europe. Other prizes are scholarships, U.S. savings bonds, sewing machines, and dress lengths of beautiful wool fabrics.

Grain

Our mountain valleys are good farming country, but the great rolling prairielands—who wanted them? For years the world took it for granted that crops wouldn't grow there.

Then suddenly, in the early 1900's, the world was told that eastern Montana was the next best thing to the Garden of Eden, that almost any farmer could get rich there. And the land was free. Under the Enlarged Homestead Act of 1909, the head of a family or anyone over twenty-one could claim 320 acres of land. A homesteader was required to build a house (a shack would do) to live in, and he had to cultivate part of the acreage for grain production.

A great influx of homesteaders poured into Montana in 1911, dazzled by promises of big crops on free land. James J. Hill, who built the Great Northern Railroad, made the promises and believed them himself. His railroad offered low fares from St. Paul and Minneapolis. For $50 a settler could rent a whole boxcar to carry his farm machinery, household goods, livestock, and lumber to eastern Montana.

The phrase "doing a land-office business" had real meaning. Professional "locators" charged $20 for taking newcomers out to choose their land. The ideal claim had trees for fuel and a stream for water, but ideal claims were few. Some homesteaders had to haul wood and water for miles by wagon.

Some of the settlers were experienced farmers, but many were not. Hundreds of single women took up claims, hired help to do the required improvement work, and expected to sell the land at good prices after they "proved up" on it.

Towns boomed along the railroad to supply the farmers' needs. Many family men left their wives and children on the claim while they lived in town to work in order to buy groceries.

In the ten years following 1909, the cultivated land in Montana increased from 258,000 acres to 3,417,000 acres. The situation looked rosy. There was plenty of rain. In 1916 farmers in one area raised 80 bushels of wheat to the acre. The average was 25.

Then disaster struck. There was no rain. In 1919 wheatlands averaged only 2.4 bushels an acre. The dry soil blew away on the unending wind. By 1925 half of Montana's farmers had lost their farms because they could not repay money they had borrowed from the banks, and a third of the banks had gone out of business.

Ed Lister told me about coming to Montana as a teen-ager to help his homesteading older brother. They raised flax (a good crop on freshly broken ground), a few cattle, some wheat and other grain. But cash was scarce.

"Everybody we knew was broke," he recalls. "We had a six-horse team but no money. Single men got together and cut each other's hair, and we often turned up for Sunday dinner on a claim where a married homesteader's wife was a good cook.

"There was a good-hearted storeowner who gave everybody credit, but his store burned, and then food got awfully scarce. When we were really broke, we made mush of ground-up wheat but had no sugar or milk to put on it.

"Four young fellows contracted to haul a big lot of hogs, and they took turns at it—because whoever delivered a load of them got a free meal from the buyer."

The drought was bad enough for young, single men, but men with

57

families had a harder time. Almost all of them gave up and moved away, bitterly disappointed and disillusioned.

The few homesteaders who had money enough to tough it out learned some important lessons. One of them was that 320 acres of prairie is not enough. Grain farming in eastern Montana has to be big. And you have to face the fact that wet years and drought years go in cycles that cannot be predicted. You can't depend on rain, but what moisture there is, you must learn how to use.

From the bitter lesson of getting along with unpredictable rainfall developed the technique of dryland farming. On reclamation projects, of course, grain farmers can irrigate, flooding their land at stated intervals with water than runs through ditches.

Dryland farming is different. A dryland farmer has to have twice as much land as he will use in a season. Half of it is summer-fallowed but not seeded. Summer fallowing means that the fields he harvested in the fall he then roughs up with big equipment to keep the weeds down and to conserve all the rain and snow that comes. He doesn't plant any grain there at all until the next year.

Dryland farming techniques have brought big changes. Years ago, farmers burned the straw that remained after the grain was threshed. The great heaps of golden straw just seemed to be in the way. In central Montana's "breadbasket" country, the skies glowed at night with the light of straw fires. Now, however, we *use* straw by stubble mulching. Farmers leave the straw and stubble on the land to hold the soil in place against the wind and to hold the moisture from whatever rain and snow may fall. This is the best way found so far to get a crop in the plains country, where the annual rainfall may be only 10 inches.

Stubble mulching involves the use of implements that don't turn the soil upside down, as a plow does, but loosen it below the surface. The stubble and straw stay on top, but the soil is loose enough for the seed to be planted with a machine called a drill.

The unending wind of the prairie has to be reckoned with. Where the wind blows hard and long, and the soil is sandy, grain growers use an additional safeguard besides stubble mulching. They strip farm. Sandy soil blows away. Strip farming prevents this loss.

Strip farming

When you're traveling by air over Montana, you see miles of strip farming, beautiful enough to make you catch your breath. The broad strips of growing grain are green in the spring and golden at harvesttime. Alternating with them are the brown strips of summer fallow. They're so even and neat that you wonder how the huge machinery of grain farming can be manipulated to form that handsome pattern. A strip may be 10 rods wide or 20 rods wide, depending on the farmer. (A rod is 5½ yards, 16½ feet.)

If the prevailing wind is from the west, strips run north and south. Then if the soil blows off the summer fallow strips of your land, your growing grain catches it. Otherwise, it might come to rest temporarily on your neighbor's land and, in a bad year, go clear to the Missouri River and add, finally, to the accumulation of useless silt that forms the Mississippi Delta.

Grain farming is big business now. It has to be. The homestead claims that couldn't be made to pay were only 320 acres, half a section—that is, half a square mile. Clarence Patrick, who raises wheat on three sections (almost 2,000 acres) near Rudyard, told me this: "The bigger we get, the less we have to depend on hiring help. Men are hard to get. I have such big machinery now that I can do the whole job myself. My old tractor was forty or fifty horsepower. The new one is one hundred and fifteen horsepower."

Mr. Patrick has his own combine to cut the grain and thresh it as the huge machine moves along the strips. He hires transient labor for the harvest, and all over the wheat country, farmers' wives and older children drive trucks to haul the threshed grain away.

The Patricks, like many wheat farmers, don't live on the farm in the winter. They lock the house and take the family to a town where the youngsters can attend a good school.

There's nothing to keep them at home after Mr. Patrick plants his fall wheat after the harvest. He hasn't got a horse or a milch cow or even a flock of chickens on the place to worry about. The fall wheat will grow for a while with no attention from him, then rest during the winter and grow again in the spring.

Along about April, he moves back to the ranch and seeds his spring wheat, and the family follows when school is out. Both crops of wheat will be ready to harvest at about the same time.

The Patrick farm is comfortably prosperous, but it's not one of the biggest. On a really big spread, a dozen huge combines may be in sight all at once, harvesting and threshing grain.

The *average* grain farm is worth more than $100,000. Thirty years ago the average value was only $7,400.

Not all ranchers specialize. Six miles south of Bainville, the William Harmon Farms raise Angus cattle, Targhee sheep, and hay and grain. They operate 14,000 acres. The family started with only 640 acres in 1929.

Prairie Montana, where our pioneers used to think nothing would grow, amounted to something after all. Three-quarters of a bushel of seed wheat to the acre is enough to plant, although in some states east of us three times as much may be needed. Our soil and our cool nights make the plants "stool out," multiply, to produce good returns from the seed planted.

Clarence Patrick plants in strips, and he stubble mulches. One spring there was no rain at all during the growing season, when most of the precipitation can be expected, but he averaged a yield of 28 bushels to the acre anyway.

Many grain growers don't own their own combines (such a machine costs about $10,000 and up) but depend on the custom combines that work up into Montana from the south, where harvest comes earlier. One man operates a combine, cutting grain in a swath 18 feet wide or more. The same machine threshes out the grain as it rolls along.

The value of wheatland keeps going up, and farms keep getting bigger and fewer, because the bigger a grain farm is, the more economical it is to operate. One tractor may cost $36,000 and pull equipment 92 feet wide. It can do a lot of work.

In one recent five-year period, the total cultivated acreage in Montana didn't change, but the total number of farms decreased by 1,939—from 28,959 to 27,020—and the average size increased to 2,437 from 2,213 acres. What happened was that some grain growers retired and sold out to their neighbors.

Grain farming is a gamble. A heavy hailstorm can wipe out a good crop in an hour. If there's too much rain—and that *can* happen—root rot may cause the growing grain simply to fall flat, which makes harvesting difficult and slow. Or it may fall just because it's top-heavy.

Montana's wheat travels far from home to its markets. Vast quantities of it move to the Orient, where millions of people used to depend entirely on rice. Japan and the Philippines buy our high-protein grain for flour. Their bakeries are small, without air conditioning, and they need high-protein flour to make the dough rise properly.

Our big competitors in supplying high-protein grain are Argentina, Canada, and Australia. The United States government pays exporters a subsidy of about 23 cents a bushel at West Coast ports so they can buy our grain for shipment. In one six-month period, Japan alone bought 12,500,000 bushels.

Our wheat country is mirage country. A farmer may notice, without being disturbed about it, that his neighbor's house, normally out of sight, has moved several miles closer to him and is hanging upside down. Or strip-farmed acres 20 miles away suddenly appear, up in the air.

In central Montana I once saw a fine big lake with a broken shoreline and two little buildings on the near side. They ran along as fast as my car moved. I never found out where that lake really is, but it certainly isn't *there*.

Chapter 4

From Hither to Yon

Transportation—stodgy word, isn't it? But transportation becomes a dramatic challenge if you want to get from hither to yon
and something is in the way.

Our mountains were in the way at our beginnings. They're still
right where they always were but not much of an obstacle anymore.
You can drive now on good highways across the Continental Divide
at several points without realizing, unless you notice a signboard,
that you have crossed the backbone of North America.

Distance is still an obstacle unless you fly. My neighbor Mary
Stevenson drove out to the airport one morning, boarded her own
plane, and flew 400 miles to Swift Current, Saskatchewan, to attend
a luncheon meeting of licensed women pilots. She was home in time
to prepare the evening meal for her family.

But not everybody or everything can go by air. Most of what we

Keelboat on the Missouri, from Big Sky *production*

sell to the world is bulky and heavy: metal products, grain, livestock, lumber. It goes out in vast quantities, mostly by railroad rather than in big trucks. One railroad car can carry almost 200,000 pounds of grain that can be unloaded in a few minutes.

Montana's major markets are far away: Chicago, the Ohio Valley, the Mississippi Valley, and the East Coast. What we sell is no more valuable to the buyer than a similar product that originates closer to those markets. We have to sell it at competitive prices even after we pay to move it. So reasonable freight rates are of great importance.

Rivers were our first highways, carrying a tremendous traffic in boats ingeniously built for special purposes. A dugout canoe, made of a hollowed-out cottonwood log, could carry several men crowded in with bales of furs. Two dugouts, lashed together and decked over, made a pirogue. Using both oars and a sail, a pirogue could go either up or down a river.

A mackinaw was a bigger boat, as much as 50 feet long, made of heavy boards, carrying as much as 15 tons of freight. Mackinaws were used only for downstream travel, and when the water was high in the spring, they might make 100 miles in a day.

A keelboat was even bigger—60 or 70 feet long. It used oars and sails, but upstream, against the current, it used manpower. The men cordelled a keelboat, clambering along the shore or wading in the water and pulling on ropes.

Then came luxury—steamboats built especially for shallow water, of which the Missouri River had plenty. Nobody has ever had a kind word to say about the treacherous Big Muddy. One comment was: "Of all the variable things in creation, the most uncertain are the action of a jury, the state of a woman's mind, and the condition of the Missouri River."

But there it was, the frontier's main highway, 2,714 miles long from its source in Montana to its meeting place with the Mississippi a few miles above St. Louis, and for most of that distance it was navigable. The Mississippi is called the Father of Waters, but let me point with pardonable pride to the fact that *our* river, the Missouri, is more than twice as long.

The Yellowstone carried some traffic, too; it flows into the Mis-

Two railroads and a highway follow the course of the Jefferson River.

souri just east of the boundary we share with North Dakota. But the Missouri was *the* river. And Fort Benton, the oldest living town in Montana, was its wild and roaring farthest port.

Fort Benton started in 1847 as a fur-trading post. It's peaceful now, even sleepy, but in its younger days it jumped with the excitement of fur traders, merchants, Indians, and whiskey runners, who smuggled liquor up into Canada.

The first steamboat that managed to reach Fort Benton did it in 1860, even before the big rush to the gold gulches. Steamboats brought up merchandise, food supplies, and adventurers. They took back furs and tanned buffalo hides and treasure from the mines after there were mines. In 1867 one boat carried raw gold worth $1,250,000.

Steamboat travel was relatively comfortable and safe. Relatively, remember. Men passengers sometimes fought off Indians who attacked from the shore. Steamboats got stuck on sandbars, were delayed by wind, had to stop to take on wood for fuel to run the boilers.

But compared with stagecoach travel, steamboating was luxurious. It was also slow. Boats had to fight the river current going upstream, and the journey from St. Joseph, Missouri, to Fort Benton took two and a half months. Going downstream was much faster.

River travel was expensive in either direction. One traveler who kept a journal told of going by steamboat from Fort Benton down to St. Louis for $100 fare. This may not seem like much now, but that's the same amount it cost him a little later for a second-class passage from New York clear across the Atlantic Ocean to Europe.

We don't put up with the vagaries of the Missouri River for travel anymore. We couldn't even if we wanted to—there are dams in the way. Nobody grieves for the good old days. Even now, it's not easy to cross the Missouri. We seldom cross by boat; we drive to the nearest bridge. There is just one bridge between Fort Benton and Fort Peck, and those towns are more than 300 miles apart.

Overland travel, especially in the mountains, was difficult when our state was being hacked out of the wilderness. Thousands of people in the gold camps came close to starving in the winter of 1864–65, because snow came early that fall. Oxteams hauling wagons freighted with needed food supplies could not get across the divide from the south and west. They were blocked by impassable drifts. Flour became so scarce that the price went up to a dollar a pound in the mining camps. Many men lived through that winter on nothing but beef and coffee so that the women and children could have bread. When the flour wagons began to come through in April, crowds of people greeted them, cheering and weeping.

Moving freight was a big problem. Montana needed everything. Somebody got the idea that camels might be just the thing for carrying freight. A man brought six camels to Virginia City, but they scared the wits out of all the horses, so he was persuaded to take them elsewhere. He lost track of one of them, and several months later a miner, out hunting for fresh meat, shot it. That camel was the funniest-looking elk he ever saw.

We got our first important road—a very rough one—because the Army needed to move troops across the Rocky Mountains to the Oregon country, where settlers needed protection from the Indians. This was the Mullan Road, from Fort Benton (troops got that far by Missouri River steamboats) to Walla Walla, Washington. Lieutenant John Mullan's crew cut the road through 624 miles of wilderness, 120 miles of it heavy forest, and it was usable for wagons in the late summer of 1860. Then troops and their equipment could reach the more settled Oregon country without going clear down around the tip of South America by ship.

While the major purpose of the Mullan Road was to move men and freight through Montana, moving them *into* Montana became important after gold was discovered. Most wagons carrying freight and pioneer families came through Idaho and had to cross the Rocky Mountains twice. A way had to be found to avoid the difficulties of crossing those mountains, and John Bozeman and John M. Jacobs found it. They blazed an easier access route (that is, they marked it but didn't clear it) north and west from a place on the Oregon Trail about 100 miles west of Fort Laramie, Wyoming. The obstacle along the Bozeman Trail was Indians.

Mountains just sit there and defy you silently, but the angry Sioux and Cheyennes took violent action against travelers, because the

Fort Howes, Custer National Forest

"Bob" Johnson

Bozeman Trail went right through their best buffalo-hunting grounds, which the government had promised them in a solemn treaty.

The Army built three forts along that trail so that soldiers could protect wagon trains, but the soldiers could barely protect even themselves. After two years of bloody battles, the government made another treaty with the Sioux and closed the Bozeman Trail in 1868. Before the troops were out of sight, the triumphant Indians set fire to the forts. The "Bozeman Massacre" in 1867 caused panic all over Montana. It really wasn't much of a massacre; only John Bozeman was killed. But everybody in the territory was sure that the Indians were going to kill all the white men.

Montana got its first railroad, a short one that came up from the south, in 1880. The first railroad that went clear across our state was the Northern Pacific, completed in 1883. The Great Northern crossed the state farther north, ten years later. New towns sprang up along the tracks of both of them. Then people and freight could get in and out, and the Missouri River wasn't our major highway anymore.

There are always people who can see problems. People who can solve the problems are scarcer. A man who for years has been solving the problem of getting from hither to yon in country that looks impossible is Robert Johnson. He learned to fly in 1923, bought a plane, then another, and built up the biggest, best-equipped privately owned flying service in the world. Its headquarters is in Missoula.

When I asked him how many planes he had, he replied with a smile, "I haven't counted my chickens lately. Somewhere between forty and fifty fixed-wing aircraft and helicopters."

Johnson Flying Service pioneered in solving a lot of emergency problems, especially for the U.S. Forest Service. Johnson pilots deliver smoke jumpers, who parachute down to fight forest fires; they rescue injured fire fighters and hunters with helicopters that don't need landing strips; they deliver food and equipment. They drop loads of chemicals on roaring fires in the mountain forests. They spray forests to control insect pests and prairie areas to kill sagebrush and make new range for cattle.

Bob Johnson trains his pilots for their specialized work. They have to know the mountain peaks and canyons, because sometimes they have to shop around through towering clouds of smoke to find a place to drop their cargoes.

On one memorable occasion a Johnson pilot even flew two horses to an isolated ranger station where the snow was deep. A veterinarian gave them a shot to put them to sleep and went along on the trip to make sure the animals didn't wake up and start tearing around in the Ford Tri-Motor that transported them.

Bob Johnson's planes work far from home—in Michigan, Minnesota, and New Mexico, for instance. He keeps finding new solutions to problems of moving things. One of our public utility firms had to set some power poles on a steep hillside in the winter, and there was no road by which a truck could take them. A Johnson "chopper" carried the poles to the spot, where the holes had already been dug for them, and workmen set up one pole every five minutes.

Chapter 5

The Forest Goes On and On

Montana has a lot of forests, some privately owned by lumber companies or ranchers and some owned by you and me—that is, national and state forests. Producing lumber is one of our major industries, because we have so much timber all over our mountains. Growing trees are timber; cut down and sawed into useful shapes of wood, they become lumber, one of our big crops.

Harvesting timber has changed tremendously since rough, tough muscle men called lumberjacks stayed out in the woods all winter, living in log bunkhouses, cutting down trees for wages, seldom taking a bath or changing their underwear. They felled trees, using axes and two-man saws, and dragged the logs to a riverbank.

Come spring, they drove the river—that is, they shoved the logs into it and let the current shoot them down to a sawmill. Then, their winter's labors ended, the lumberjacks went roaring into town, took

Engelmann spruce

a bath, bought clean clothes, and got drunk, but not necessarily in that order.

All this has changed. Lumberjacks are called loggers now, and most of them are solid family men who drive into the woods in the morning to work and drive home again for supper. They have wives and families, and they're just as concerned as other citizens about making sure the children do their homework.

They don't fell trees in the old way, either, with man-powered saws. In preparing to fell a tree, a logger chops a notch in the trunk on the side toward which he wants the tree to fall. Then, on the opposite side, a little above the notch, he uses a motor-drive portable chain saw to cut through the trunk.

The old-time lumberjacks' legendary hero, Paul Bunyan, wouldn't be able to earn a living in the woods these days without learning new techniques. Much of the work that used to require muscle power (of men or mules or oxen) is done by huge machines today.

Lumberjacks used to work mostly in the winter, but the sawmills were closed down then. Present-day loggers work all year round, and so do the mills that make lumber. In the summer, many loggers move out into the mountains with their families, living in small trailer houses or pickup campers, and the youngsters love it.

In a few places, and there will be more of them, loggers go to work in helicopters because it's faster than driving a car over rough, snow-drifted roads.

Loggers do not, of course, simply head into the woods and start cutting down trees just any old place. The timber belongs to somebody, and whether it is publicly or privately owned, it is scientifically managed by expert foresters. Timber harvest has to be carefully planned, taking into consideration not only the lumber that will be produced from a specified area but also protection of watersheds and the grazing needs of animals.

The University of Montana in Missoula includes a School of Forestry that trains specialists in many fields, including forest management. It's a tough course because there is so much for a man to learn, and getting through it requires a minimum of four years and usually a little more.

Lumberjacks, early 1900's

Trees are attacked by various insect pests that do a lot of damage. Foresters have to figure out what to do about tree diseases, forest fires, and building access roads into the woods.

The Northern Region of the U.S. Forest Service has headquarters in Missoula. Activities are coordinated there for 26,000,000 acres of national forests in Montana, eastern Washington, northern Idaho, North Dakota, and western South Dakota.

The government offers certain areas of stumpage—merchantable trees—for sale to lumber companies. Timber cruisers measure the trees and estimate how many board feet they will produce. A board foot is one foot wide, one foot long, and one inch thick—not that anybody hacks up lumber into such sizes on purpose; it's just a way of measuring.

Lumber companies bid for the stumpage, and the highest bidder gets it. Then the lumber company, which operates one or more sawmills, gets bids from contract loggers to cut down the trees and deliver the logs. Contract loggers (sometimes called gyppo loggers) are rugged outdoorsmen, in business for themselves. They sometimes make a lot of money; sometimes they go broke. A contract logger has his own money invested in huge, expensive machinery for building roads and loading and hauling logs. He makes his own contracts with loggers who do the actual cutting and loading.

Our trees are soft wood: Douglas fir, lodgepole pine, Ponderosa pine, Engelmann spruce, and western larch, or tamarack. They are all conifers—that is, their seeds grow in cones.

Airplane passengers, flying over the mountains, sometimes wring their hands at the sight of bare patches where the timber has all been cut off. "Ruining the forests!" some passengers moan. But they're wrong. Clear cutting is the best way to harvest much of the timber that grows in Montana. And harvesting is exactly what we do with trees. Cut one down, and it's gone—but another one will grow. And with clear cutting we get even-aged forests, all the trees the same age and about the same size.

In an uneven-aged forest, trees are of many sizes, and seedlings have to struggle to live. Seedlings of the species we have don't do well in the shade. They need light, and when they all start at the same time, they have an equal chance for survival.

A tree three or four hundred years old may be only a few inches in diameter if it has always had to compete for moisture and space. Trees that are to be used to the best advantage need room. In a

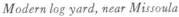
Modern log yard, near Missoula

stagnant forest—one that isn't cared for—as much timber dies as there is growing, and the dead timber has no value.

An uneven-aged forest looks good from a distance, but it's dark in there, and after a rain it stays damp for a long time. Flowers are few. The ground is covered with needles and twigs and branches and the rotting logs of trees that matured and died and fell every which way. A thick forest doesn't provide good browse for deer or elk, and if fire strikes it, getting the fire under control among the downed timber is very hard indeed.

Conservation is not the same as preservation. Conservation includes the *use* of natural resources. Forests provide more than just trees to cut down and manufacture into lumber. Our forests are used for many purposes: recreation (camping, hiking, picnics), hunting birds and big game, stream and lake fishing, water sports, winter sports, and just plain looking at. They protect the water supply of many towns, too.

In a well-managed forest, trees for the future are not left entirely to nature. Foresters plant seedlings in the ground or scatter seeds from low-flying planes. Birds like the seeds very well, and porcupines love to nibble baby trees, but foresters use chemical repellents to discourage this lunching.

Foresters at work

Harvesting timber is a long-term proposition. A man who plants trees that will grow in a clear-cut area will be only a memory when those trees are mature and ready to cut, ninety to one hundred years later. Men of his grandchildren's generation will harvest them.

Some of our forest land is owned by lumber companies. The biggest forest owner in Montana (aside from you and me with our national forests) is the Northern Pacific Railroad, which operates the Plum Creek lumber mills at Pablo and Columbia Falls. Anaconda Forest Products, a division of the Anaconda Company, is next; then the St. Regis Paper Company. Glacier Park Company is a big timber owner but has no mill of its own. Intermountain Lumber Company is a big producer of lumber but, unlike the others, doesn't own any forests. Intermountain buys its timber from the U.S. Forest Service.

The Anaconda Company got into the lumber business many years ago because of its need for mine timbers. Whole forests have been buried in the copper mines at Butte. Some of the old timbers come to light again as the Berkeley Pit increases its dimensions.

Forest fire is an ever-present danger in dry weather. The summer of 1967 will go down in history as a really bad one. Between August 11 and September 11, an average of twenty-five new fires broke out *every day* in the Forest Service's Northern Region. Missoula, center of fire-fighting activities for the whole region, was a busy city. The sky usually had at least one plane or helicopter in sight at any time during any day, because air transportation is vital in fighting forest fires.

Thirty thousand men, all told, flew out in a total of 134 planes and 42 helicopters. Twenty-nine air tankers dropped tons of fire retardant to discourage the windswept flames.

The Sundance fire, in Idaho, raced 21 miles in one day and burned a square mile of mature timber every few minutes. That one took a month to control. It burned 23,500 acres of national forest and 32,410 acres of other land, and for a while 2,261 men were working on it all at once, supported by fourteen helicopters. The heat was so intense that it ruined a bridge by melting quarter-inch reinforced steel.

During that terrible summer, any man who looked reasonably

healthy was likely to be firmly invited to join a fire crew whether he was enthusiastic about the idea or not. Crack fire-fighting crews from twenty-seven Indian tribes in many states came in by plane. After two bad fires in Glacier National Park were controlled, somebody had to rush to the nearest town to buy $6 worth of shampoo so that the Indians with long braids could get cleaned up.

From Alaska, 120 Eskimos were flown into Montana. The Forest Service feeds its fire fighters well, but these men had a special problem. They were accustomed to smoked salmon as their staple diet. A big shipment of it reached their camp, but they had been moved to another one, where they had to eat T-bone steaks.

Some of us think the rain dance of the southwestern Indian tribes should be subsidized by the government. In Hamilton, two Zuñis put on a rain dance, and the next day that area had rain that was virtually a cloudburst.

Among the fire fighters were a lot of bold young men known as smoke jumpers. They parachute out of planes to attack fires. I asked one of them, "Why do you volunteer for this kind of work? It looks dangerous to me."

He replied, "Well, I always did want to jump out of airplanes."

Most jumpers are college students, and there are more applicants for these dramatic jobs than there are openings to be filled. A jumper must be between eighteen and twenty-eight years old, be accustomed to rugged outdoor life, weigh not more than 180 pounds, and pass a rigid physical examination. Candidates must have at least one season's experience in fighting fires.

They get four weeks of training in parachute jumping, fire fighting, calisthenics, and first aid. They learn how to fall safely—and, of course, how to fight fire when they reach the ground. Sometimes walking back to civilization after the job is done is harder than doing the job, and it is certainly more tedious.

The largest of the eight smoke jumper bases in the United States is in Missoula. It is headquarters for more than 150 airborne fire fighters. (Idaho has three bases; Washington, California, Oregon, and New Mexico each have one.)

Here's an example of the usefulness of jumpers: A fire was spotted

1

2

1. Forest fire

2. Training for
   parachute jumping

3. Smokey the Bear
   fire prevention sign

4 and 5. Smoke jumping

6. Fighting the fire

4

3

5

6

building up in the Selway Wilderness Area of the Bitterroot National Forest—one of the most inaccessible spots in the United States. A man on foot, or even riding a horse, would need two days to get there. But three jumpers dropped under the billowing canopies of their chutes, and five minutes after they hit the ground they were attacking the fire scientifically. In two hours they had it extinguished.

Jumpers bail out at about 1,500 feet. They wear two chutes, one for emergency use if the other one doesn't open. Their tools, food, and other equipment are dropped by separate parachutes. Obviously, the pilots who do the dropping are specially trained experts.

The present Aerial Fire Depot, seven miles from Missoula, was dedicated in 1954 by President Dwight D. Eisenhower. The reason it's there is that Missoula is the geographic center of the Northern Region, which includes about 8,000,000 acres of forest with no roads. Another reason why Missoula was selected as the logical place for smoke jumper training and activities is that Johnson Flying Service was there already.

Timber burned in a forest fire is not completely destroyed. Much

Forest destroyed by fire

of it can be harvested and used for lumber, but this has to be done within a year; otherwise, the timber cracks and gets insects in it that spread to live trees and damage them. The forest land that was burned over in the bad summer of 1967 was seeded to grass right after the first heavy rain to reduce soil loss and retard water runoff.

Smokey the Bear, symbol of forest fire prevention, says, "Only you can prevent forest fires." It's something to think about—the reminder keeps us alert. But it's not true. Of the 1,838 fires that ravaged Northern Region forests in 1967, only 414 were caused by people. The other 1,424 were the result of lightning.

Another point about the Smokey the Bear promotion is that sometimes you see him protectively carrying a baby fawn or some other helpless creature, and this gives you the idea that bears are friendly creatures. Never forget that bears are *dangerous*. Grizzly bears are vicious: They kill fawns and sometimes human beings. Black bears, which you may see in Glacier and Yellowstone national parks, certainly *act* friendly. They sit along the roads, begging for sandwiches. But if you are so stupid as to hand out food, or to try to pet one of these tame-looking beasts, you can very well end up screaming, scarred for life, and maybe minus a hand.

Not all the forest lands that you and I own are used for harvesting timber. Some especially beautiful mountain vastnesses have been set aside to remain wonderful and untouched as wilderness areas, so that we and future generations can see what the country was like before man ever set foot in it. These are wilderness areas, different from national parks.

In a wilderness area, there can be no commercial timber cutting, no roads, no permanent habitations. There are trails for hikers and horseback riders, and for horses or mules that carry camping equipment, but wheeled vehicles are forbidden. Man is welcome only as a visitor, to camp and hunt and fish—but not to stay.

Wilderness areas are unspoiled grandeur, with blue mountain lakes and high alpine meadows and towering peaks. By Congressional action, they have been set aside as a kind of national treasure. Every visitor takes some of the treasure home in his own heart without diminishing the magnificent whole.

81

Chapter 6

The Pleasures of Montana

Snow

We have plenty of room and plenty of interesting things to do and see in Montana. Several years ago, somebody realized that you can do something with snow besides grumble about it, so now we have lots of skiing. The ideal situation, of course, would be to have snow on the ski runs but no snow on the streets in town, but we haven't yet figured out how to arrange this.

A world-famous ski resort, where national championship races are often held, is the Big Mountain, a few miles north of Whitefish. There are dozens of other ski runs around the state, too.

And there is a newer winter sport, luge, which became an official Olympic Games event in 1964. The first luge run in North America was built at Lolo Hot Springs in western Montana in 1965. It's a steep, twisting course 3,200 feet long.

A luge is a peculiar sled with steel runners. A luge racer lies

Snow ranger skiing

almost flat on his back, raising his head just enough to see where he's going—and he goes at 50 miles an hour or more. He steers by pushing his toes against the runners and by pulling a short rope.

Fishing

We can keep busy with outdoor sports all year round. Fishing, for instance.

For more than fifty years we've been wondering about a mysterious monster fish that people keep seeing in Flathead Lake. The people who have reported and described it were cold sober, and some of them were pretty scared. The Flathead Lake monster has plenty of room in that great big beautiful lake, 28 miles long and 7 miles wide. The monster has sometimes been described as a sea serpent, with a head the size of a horse's head.

Sight of it has frightened visitors who hadn't even heard of the creature, so they couldn't have been expecting to get a glimpse of it. Some of them run for their cameras, but nobody has got a picture of the monster. Some of them run for a rifle, but the monster swims merrily on and disappears behind an island. What's so startling about it is that it doesn't stay underwater like a proper fish. It sometimes swims with its back above the surface, and that's why people notice it. Just about every summer somebody reports having glimpsed this peculiar something, so it must be more than just a legend.

Fish of more manageable sizes abound in our lakes and streams: whitefish, kokanee salmon, grayling, perch, bass, and many kinds of trout—brown, rainbow, cutthroat, Dolly Varden, golden, eastern brook, and lake.

Great big mackinaw trout grow in Whitefish Lake, by accident. Years ago some tanks of baby fish were dumped from a railroad car into the lake because all the fish seemed to be dead and spoiling. But there were survivors, and they grew and multiplied. A few years later, fishermen began to catch big fish of a kind that wasn't supposed to be there at all, and now mackinaws are a big drawing card.

A friend of mine, fishing for macks for the first time, hooked one

84

A good catch

—and then his small boat turned over when a big wave hit it side-ways. The time was late winter, the water was bitter cold, and he and his companion came close to drowning, but the first thing he said when another boat came to the rescue was "Don't lose that fish!" Well, that's how dedicated some fishermen are.

Montana has eight rivers, or stretches of river, that are classified as blue ribbon trout streams. Nobody really goes out and pins blue rib-bons on running water, of course. Streams are rated in five classes by a Stream Classification Committee of experts on the basis of how easy they are to reach, how good they are to look at, and how productive they are. Class 1 streams are blue ribbon—identified with blue on an official map—and Montana has 452 miles of them. They are classed as having national as well as statewide value for fishermen.

Montana boasts of two aquatic creatures (in addition to the mysterious Flathead monster) that are rare indeed. One is a great big paddlefish, or spoonbill cat, sometimes caught in the Missouri River drainage. The only other place they're found in the world is in the Yangtze River in China. Somebody hauled one in from Fort Peck Lake that weighed 120 pounds.

That lake is the largest single body of water in Montana—189 miles long when it's full—and it was formed when Fort Peck Dam was built on the Missouri River. The dam provides power and helps control floods downstream on the tricky Big Muddy.

The Madison River is one of the finest fishing streams you'll find anywhere. Its course includes a lake five miles long that was created in August, 1959, by one of the severest earthquakes ever recorded in the United States. On the night of August 17, the earth shook,

Badlands, Makoshika State Park

and the side of a mountain, a few miles northwest of West Yellowstone, broke off, roared down, and filled three-quarters of a mile of the Madison River Canyon. Earthquake Lake resulted.

Nineteen of the 250 people who were camping in the area were covered by that terrible avalanche of earth and rocks, and 9 more died of injuries. Exactly a year later, a memorial plaque was dedicated on an immense boulder that had come to rest after flying from the other side of the river. When you stand and read that plaque, you are uncomfortably aware that you are standing on the grave of 19 people who were swallowed up by the earthquake.

Half a million people visit the Earthquake Area each summer to marvel at the great scars left on the mountains and to relax in the new campgrounds that the Forest Service has built along there. On top of the slide is an earthquake-proof visitors center with educational exhibits.

Earth Formations

Some people like to explore caves. They are called spelunkers. Some people detest being underground. They are called scaredy-cats, and I'm one of them. Being in a cave makes me feel that I'm holding up a whole mountain all by myself, and it's simply too much responsibility.

But most of the 60,000 tourists who go through the Lewis and Clark Caverns, near Whitehall, every summer enjoy the experience more than I did. The trip takes an hour and a half, and it's spectacular, with strange formations to stare at and a guide to explain them. There are immense stone icicles called stalactites, and upside-down stone icicles called stalagmites. The nicest thing about the place, from my point of view, is that it has electric lights. It's air-conditioned by nature, with a temperature of 46 degrees.

Meriwether Lewis and William Clark never saw the caverns, but we tend to name things for them anyway. A couple of ranchers found the entrance almost ninety years after Lewis and Clark didn't. The area is a state park.

Another place with peculiar natural formations—but these are out in the open—is Makoshika State Park, near Glendive. This is spectacular badlands country, called badlands because it's no good for anything except to look at. Makoshika is a Sioux Indian word that's supposed to mean "hell cooled over." Really, the formations are of limestone eroded into strange shapes by wind and water.

Montana has twenty-six state parks and recreation areas, all remarkable for something interesting.

Dude Ranches and Rodeos

Montana has many dude ranches. By no means all of them are working cattle ranches. Any summer resort that provides room, board, and a horse to ride can bill itself as a dude ranch, even if it doesn't have a cow on the place.

A dude is a person who comes West from somewhere else and·intends to go back there. A tenderfoot, in contrast, is a newcomer who is bewildered but plans to stay. Neither term is derogatory. A dude wrangler is a cowboy who herds dudes around. He helps boost them into the saddle, swings down off his horse to open and shut the gate, and baffles guests by using words like *cavvy* (the whole bunch of horses at the ranch) and *bronc stomper* (a rider who is unnecessarily rough with his mount).

The wrangler may confuse you by remarking, "I'm a dally welter," or, "I'm a tie-fast man." This refers to his preferred method of roping. A tie-fast man fastens one end of his throw rope (he may call it a lariat) to the horn of his stock saddle—but if a big steer in his loop jumps hard and the saddle cinch breaks, the roper goes flying and may be badly injured.

A dally welter holds the loose end of his rope in his left hand, throws his loop, and then speedily "takes his dallies," wrapping the loose end around his saddle horn. His saddle won't get jerked off his horse—but if he gets his thumb caught while wrapping the rope around the horn, he may lose that thumb. If you see a cowboy or a cattleman with his left thumb missing or mutilated, he's a **dally welter**.

A Western saddle does have a horn, properly called a pommel.

88

Dude ranchers, Gallatin Forest trail

It's not to make a noise with; it's a leather-covered projection, and the first thing a dude finds out is that it's handy to grab hold of when the horse starts to trot. You're not supposed to hang onto it. You're supposed to hang onto the horse by gripping your knees. But once at a rodeo I saw an Indian pickup man, a superb rider, who often rested one hand on his saddle horn, so I decided that it must be all right for me, too.

We have rodeos all over during the summer, with fine riders and mean horses. The nice thing about a rodeo is that you can cut loose and yell your head off even if you don't know what it's all about. A couple of hints: Watch the pickup men, who help yank the bucking-horse riders out of harm's way so their mounts won't kill them. And watch the clown. He's not there solely to be comical. One of his jobs is to distract the attention of the dangerous Brahma bulls after they throw their riders.

High Scenery

"Grandeur" is the word for Glacier National Park. Look down from Going-to-the-Sun Highway and you'll see slopes that look like grassy meadows—but the "grass" is trees. Look up from almost any-where, at jagged peaks and tumbled rocks, and it's good for your soul. On the top of the Continental Divide you can usually have a snow-ball fight in July, standing ankle-deep in wild flowers.

Glacier Park has glaciers, of course, and you can get to some of them without a great deal of trouble, but you do have to get out of your car and hike and climb. The National Park Service does every-thing it can to keep tourists happy, but the rangers haven't figured out how to move the glaciers down where they'll be handy for people who are too lazy to make an effort.

Part of Yellowstone National Park is in Montana, too, although most of it is in Wyoming.

Wild Animals

Montana's hunting is great. This makes hunters happy, but their wives aren't always pleased to have another elk or deer or antelope or another bunch of wild ducks or pheasants brought home tri-umphantly. A neighbor of mine, with two dedicated hunters in the family, had to buy a second food freezer to accommodate all that meat.

If we just want to look at wild animals without shooting at them, we drive to one of the national parks or to the National Bison Range at Moiese. The first time I went to the bison range, my picnic party was delighted to see several deer in the tall grass. "Shh!" said the driver as he stopped the car. "Don't scare them!"

We found we *couldn't* scare them. They tried to climb into the car with us. I pushed one doe on her patent-leather nose to keep her from gobbling a bag of candy, which is very bad for deer. When we had our picnic, another doe snatched a hamburger bun right off my plate.

What we really went there for was to see the bison. That's their proper name, but we usually call them buffaloes. Vast herds of them once roamed the prairies of the West. They were the mainstay of the Indians of the plains, who lived on their meat, and used their hides, bones, horns and tendons for all sorts of tools and coverings and decorations.

90

The bison, the biggest mammal native to North America, was almost extinct when 41 of them were collected and bought by the American Bison Society to stock the 18,540 acres of the National Bison Range, established in 1908. The land was bought from the Flathead Indians.

Bison are not gentle creatures, like deer. They're huge and stupid and dangerous. Visitors to the refuge at Moiese don't get in among them. But during the summer months there is a 19-mile self-guiding automobile tour that enables tourists to see the bison grazing on their hills and to take pictures fairly close up.

The foundation herd of 41 has increased through the years. There are calves every spring, and by October about 400 of the big animals are there. This is too many to feed through the winter, so some of them are sold after the fall roundup.

In one typical year, 55 live bison were sold to private buffalo ranchers who raise these animals for meat. These were young animals—long yearlings and long two-year-olds. (The same terms apply to cattle: A long yearling is a big calf, a few months more than a year old.)

Some of the bison are slaughtered and butchered at the refuge, and the meat is sold to clubs and organizations, usually for fund-raising dinners. It's not everybody who can claim to have eaten buf-

Bison cows and calves

Bull elk

falo meat. The Indians and fur trappers who used to live on it considered domestic beef insipid in comparison.

The bison range is home to many animals—mule deer and white-tail deer, elk, bighorn sheep and pronghorns. Pronghorn is the right name for the quick, graceful animal that most people call an antelope.

In 1933 a remarkable bison calf was born at the refuge. He was almost an albino; he was white except that he seemed to be wearing a dark brown hat between his horns. White buffalo are very rare. The Indians used to consider them sacred, so this one was given an Indian name, Big Medicine. You can still see him, but not at the bison refuge. He died at the great age of twenty-six and is now on display in the State Historical Society Museum in Helena.

Bobcat

Wild mink

Canadian geese

Porcupine

Ringtail cat

Whitetail buck deer

We have some rather spooky places, where you get a slight chill up your spine if you have just a little imagination. For example, the Pryor Mountains, on the Crow Indian reservation, are sacred to the Crows. Long ago, their legends say, they were warned that sometime those mountains would save their people. They have legends about a strange race of little people who live in the Pryors. Sometimes an Indian will make a quiet pilgrimage to a certain rock there and leave a small offering of beads as a gift to the friendly little people.

The Little Rocky Mountains, an isolated range in central Montana, have their own kind of chill up the spine because of the outlaw killings that took place there around the turn of the century. Kid Curry and his two outlaw brothers used to hide out there after committing crimes in Wyoming and other states. The brothers' last name was Logan, but we speak of them as the Curry boys—and people in the Little Rockies don't like to speak of them at all.

Kid Curry killed a pioneer settler named Pike Landusky, and then somebody killed the Kid's brother Johnnie, and then the Kid killed a man named Winters. Later the other brother, Lonnie, was shot in another state, and the Kid disappeared. But while they were in their prime, the Curry boys and some of their badmen friends perpetrated our biggest train robbery, near Malta, on the Great Northern Railroad. They got a huge amount of currency—which did them no good, because the bills hadn't been signed. There was lots of excitement, with law officers making up posses to pursue the gang, but legend says that most of the posses earnestly rode off in the wrong direction rather than catch up with those dangerous characters.

Two other spooky places are battlegrounds. The Battle of the Little Bighorn, the Custer "massacre," took place near where the town of Hardin is now. The site is a national monument. Custer isn't buried there, but the soldiers who died with him are, and so are many veterans of later wars, for this is a national cemetery. Except for the cemetery with its neat rows of white headstones, the

Custer Battlefield National Monument, Little Bighorn Valley

battleground is as bleak as it was on that hot June day in 1876 when soldiers far from home died there among the sagebrush and the prickly pear.

The Big Hole Battlefield in western Montana is another impressive place. Here, on August 9, 1877, the Army fought Chief Joseph and his Nez Percés but did not stop them. The Nez Percés were peaceable Indians who had been pushed out of their country in northeastern Oregon because white settlers wanted it. Then they were pushed out of northern Idaho.

Pursued by the military, the Indians fled, trying to reach safety in Canada. On the way, they camped in the Big Hole Valley, and there their sleeping camp was attacked by troops commanded by Colonel John Gibbon. About eighty-nine Indians were killed, only twelve of them warriors—the rest were women and children and people too old or sick to fight.

The site is now a national monument, where you can still see bullet-scarred trees and the trenches in which soldiers and warriors lay to fire at one another. There is nothing there that you can feel proud of—unless you are a Nez Percé Indian.

95

North American Indian Days celebration

The desperate Nez Percés swung down through Yellowstone National Park and then north again. They tried then to get to Canada, where the government had the reputation of treating Indians fairly. They thought they had reached safety when they camped, exhausted, in the Bear Paw Mountains—but they were 30 miles short of the international boundary. Colonel Nelson A. Miles and his troops attacked them, and they had to give up. Here Chief Joseph made a tragic speech of surrender, ending with the words, "From where the sun now stands, I will fight no more forever."

The Nez Percés had been on the run for four months and had fought their way over 1,300 miles of mountainous country. They deserved to keep their freedom, but they lost it.

Chief Joseph of the Nez Percés

Markers

Montana's historical markers along the highways are famous. Montana State Highway Commission set up 114 of them. They are signboards, always informative and sometimes funny, that tell what happened in various places. R. H. Fletcher wrote the words. For example, this sign was set up at all the places where major highways enter the state:

> You are coming into the heart of the West where you will cut a lot of mighty interesting old time trails. Just turn your fancy loose to range the coulees, gulches, prairie and mountains and if your imagination isn't hobbled you can people them with picturesque phantoms of the past.
>
> We have marked and explained many of the most interesting historical and scenic spots along the highways. Watch for them and help us to preserve these markers.
>
> Here is wishing you lots of luck and many pleasant miles in Montana.

Unfortunately, many of these interesting markers have had to be removed because of rigid rules governing signboards along the Interstate Highway. You can drive for miles without a chance to find out what you want to know about the country you're passing through.

97

Chapter 7

Colorful Characters

The most unbelievable of all Montana's colorful characters was Liver-Eating Johnson. His real name was John Johnston, and he was a mountain man, a fur trapper. He came to Montana about 1846, married a Flathead Indian girl, and returned to his cabin one day from a trapping expedition to find that she had been killed by some Crow Indians.

He swore vengeance, and he took it in a very bloody way. He made a habit of killing Crow Indians and eating their livers. (Nobody knows why he chose to eat his enemies' livers.) Liver-Eating Johnson spent years tracking down Crow Indians, killing and scalping them, and eating at least a token bite out of their livers. His tally altogether was about 300 of them! Later in his life, he became a friend of the Crow tribe. They had reason to respect him.

Once he was captured by Blackfeet Indians. He hit his guard over

Liver-Eating Johnson

the head, hacked off the man's leg, and set out through the snow to rejoin his partner at a cabin some 500 miles away. When he got there, he threw down the human leg (what was left of it; he had nothing else to eat), and asked his partner, "How you fixed for meat?"

Liver-Eating Johnson was an old man when he settled down in 1888 to a quiet job: He was the first town marshal of Red Lodge, a new coal-mining town. He was especially kind to the children there, and they adored him.

He died early in 1900 in Los Angeles.

The stories about this man are beyond belief, but if you read a book called *Crow Killer: The Saga of Liver-Eating Johnson*, you'll probably be convinced. The authors, Raymond W. Thorp and Robert Bunker, based the book on conversations they had with old men who had known the liver eater. Some of them were still afraid of him years after he was dead.

Thomas Francis Meagher

On July 1, 1867, the territorial secretary of Montana disappeared off a steamboat docked at Fort Benton. His name was Thomas Francis Meagher. He was a hot-tempered, impetuous fellow, famous around the world. He had friends and enemies—everybody who knew him was one or the other.

Tom Meagher was born in Ireland. He was an ardent revolutionary in favor of freedom for Ireland. He was so violent an orator, in fact, that Queen Victoria's government sentenced him to death for seditious libel when he was only twenty-three years old. The sentence was, however, commuted to banishment in Tasmania. He escaped from that faraway island and came to the United States.

Meagher was always a fighter. He became a brigadier general on the Union side in the Civil War. After the war ended, President Andrew Johnson appointed him secretary of Montana Territory, and because Governor Sidney Edgerton went back to the States as soon as Meagher arrived, he became acting governor.

The acting governor had a talent for making people mad. He

Thomas Francis Meagher

made many Montanans furious when he pardoned a murderer named James Daniels. Nobody but the President had the right to do this. A group of Helena vigilantes hanged Daniels (with the pardon still in his pocket) and pinned a sign to his coat: "If our acting governor does this again, we will hang him, too."

Meagher was an unhappy man when he rode into Fort Benton on what turned out to be the last day of his life. He had been sick for several days, and he told a friend that the people of the town were out to kill him. He had one nice thing to look forward to, though: His wife, who had been visiting in the East, was coming upriver on a steamboat.

That night the pilot of a steamboat that was docked at Fort Benton invited Meagher to use his own stateroom, as hotel accommodations were scarce in that brawling river port. About nine o'clock, a guard saw a figure in white plunge off the boat and heard two agonized shouts. Nothing more was ever seen or heard of General Thomas Francis Meagher, although men searched frantically along the riverbanks.

His wife arrived, to find that she was probably a widow. She offered a reward for identification of his body, but nobody ever claimed the money.

Rumors and gossip turned into legends that are still told in Montana. Years later, a so-called petrified man was exhibited in a traveling show, and many people believed that it was the body of Meagher, mysteriously preserved after drowning.

Years after that, an old man "confessed" that he had killed Meagher for pay, but the man was a notorious liar, and anyway he changed his story a few days later.

Rattlesnake Jake

Rattlesnake Jake was an obscure, unsung horse thief who became famous on the day he died, along with a companion known as Long-Haired Ed Owen, in a wild blaze of gunfire in Lewistown, Montana.

The date was July 4, 1884, and a big celebration was scheduled. The two horse thieves rode into town, not to celebrate their country's birthday but to "hooraw" (intimidate) the citizens.

Right away Rattlesnake Jake intruded in an argument between two other men and hit one of them across the mouth with his revolver. Then the two desperadoes stepped into the nearest saloon for a few drinks apiece.

When they returned to the street, Jake took a sudden dislike to a man who just happened to be there. Jake started shooting, was wounded in the right forefinger, and switched his revolver to the other hand. Then gunfire became general, and startled citizens started ducking for cover.

Jake got on his horse, grabbed his Winchester, and fired at anybody handy. Shot in the abdomen, he wheeled his horse and galloped up the street. But he rode back to help his pal, who was firing from a kneeling position. On the way, Jake killed a man named Smith by putting a bullet through his head.

Both horse thieves fell within a few minutes. Rattlesnake Jake had nine bullets in him, and Long-Haired Owen had five. The wounds were solemnly counted by men who hastily assembled for an official inquest. The three dead men were buried the next day.

Nobody mourned for the two horse thieves, but the normally peaceable men who killed them thoroughly admired one quality in them: their raw courage. Rattlesnake Jake and Long-Haired Owen were vicious and worthless, but, as a contemporary newspaper account remarked, "They fought with a bravery that was simply grand." And so they became part of our history.

Charley Russell

Even before a cowboy named Charles Marion Russell became world-famous as an artist, just about everybody liked him. After he was famous, everybody still liked him, and anyone who ever knew him, or even met him once, boasts about it to this day. I never met him, but when I was in grade school, I saw him make a speech.

"Saw" is the right word. He didn't say anything out loud. He spoke in Indian sign talk, and his wife translated. I don't remember a thing he said. What was important to the audience was that we had seen the great Charley Russell and that he talked in hand signs, as the various tribes of Plains Indians used to do.

Charley came out from Missouri in 1880 when he was about sixteen, herded sheep for a while, and then became a cowboy. He was always drawing or painting pictures of cowboys and Indians. Pictures that he gave to friends are now in immensely valuable art collections.

When he was in his early thirties, he married a girl named Nancy Cooper, who became his business manager. She saw to it that his pictures sold for high prices. After that he quit cowboying, set up a studio in Great Falls (it is a museum now), and painted as a full-time job.

Charley was only twenty-three when he painted Montana's most famous picture. He was riding for a cow outfit during the Terrible Winter of 1886–87, when stockmen lost most of their herds. He rode the range in that bitter weather, when both men and animals suffered. When his boss, who lived in town, asked for a report on the cattle, Charley got out his watercolors and answered with a picture.

103

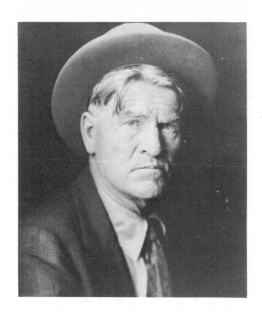
Charley Russell

It's the size of a postcard. It shows a gaunt cow about to collapse in the snow, with five wolves waiting for her to die. Charley called it "Waiting for a Chinook," but it is better known as "The Last of 5,000." It became so well known that a few years later he made a copy, slightly bigger. That one, now in the Whitney Gallery of Western Art in Cody, Wyoming, was once sold for $60,000!

The original is on display in odd-numbered years in the Montana Historical Society Museum in Helena; in even-numbered years it can be seen in the Trigg-Russell Gallery in Great Falls.

Charley Russell wrote and illustrated several books. Even the personal letters he wrote to friends are museum prizes now, because he illustrated them, too.

Montana's cowboy artist was a famous man and financially comfortable when he died in 1926. In Statuary Hall in the nation's Capitol, each state is permitted to install statues of two of its famous men. Charley Russell, the cowboy artist, is Montana's only contribution thus far.

Joseph and Molly Slade

Joseph Albert Slade was not an outlaw, but he was tough, ruthless, and hard to get along with. He finished his career at the end of a

104

hangman's rope in Virginia City, after the vigilantes had warned him to get out of town. Actually, he was hanged for disorderly conduct (very disorderly), and the vigilantes were ashamed when they cooled down and thought about it.

His wife, Molly, was intensely and even violently loyal to him. She was also smart. Before they came to the Montana gold gulches, she saved his life. A group of badmen had him locked in a cabin, with every intention of killing him, but he talked them into bringing Molly to say good-bye. She came, weeping—with two revolvers hidden under her long skirt. She and Joe came out of the cabin with guns in their hands and neatly got away.

But she was too late to save him from the vigilantes' rope. She was in their little stone house, 12 miles away, when a rider came on a sweating horse to tell her that Joe was in danger. She leaped aboard her own saddle horse and galloped down to town, screaming, with a gun in her hand and her long black hair flying.

But her beloved was already dead. She told his executioners what she thought of them, and they never forgot it. She refused to have him buried there, among his enemies, but kept his body preserved in whiskey in a metal-lined coffin until the snow melted in the spring. Then she took him to Salt Lake City for burial. Later she married the man who drove the team on that dismal journey. She separated from him eventually, and nobody knows what became of her.

There is a legend that the isolated house where the Slades were living was haunted. Travelers who passed that way said they heard, at night, the sound of galloping hooves and the screams of Molly Slade as she rode away, again and again, to try to save the man she loved.

Calamity Jane

The woman known as Calamity Jane told so many lies about herself that nobody knows where the facts stop and the fiction begins. A couple of things are certain: She was a famous Western character, and we're glad there are no more like her in Montana now.

She didn't spend all her time in Montana, by any means. She

drifted from one Western state to another, and any place she was, most people were glad to have her leave.

Her real name (maybe) was Martha Jane Canarray. She said she was born in Missouri in 1848, but maybe it was in 1844. She came to Virginia City, Montana, as a teen-ager with her parents.

Calamity Jane dressed like a man, smoked black cigars, swore like a trooper, and drank like a bottomless pit. She worked at men's jobs. She was a skilled mule skinner—teamster, that is—and very handy with a 30-foot bullwhip. Sometimes she made a living by chopping down pine trees to make fence posts. For a while, in Montana, she cooked for a bunch of horse thieves. What she *said* she did was even more spectacular.

Calamity claimed that she had been a stagecoach driver, a pony express rider, and a scout for General Custer. She said that an Army captain invented her nickname after she saved his life in a battle with Indians: He told her she was a wonderful woman to have around in a calamity. She claimed later that she was actually in the Army at the time. She really was *with* the Army once or twice, as a civilian teamster, driving mules.

Calamity really was a good woman to have around in a calamity. She had a heart of gold. There are several true stories about her kindness. When smallpox struck the wild mining camp at Deadwood, South Dakota, and nobody dared care for the sick for fear of contracting the dread disease, Calamity took over. She moved into the isolated pesthouse, fed and bathed the sufferers, and washed their clothes.

She married once or twice and had a couple of children. One was a daughter who died in 1951.

The love of Calamity's life was Wild Bill Hickok, a famous gunman and gambler. She said she married him, but the daughter she claimed was his was born three years before she met him. Anyway, Wild Bill already had a wife.

But once Calamity met him, she followed him around like an adoring puppy. Wild Bill was shot in the back while playing poker. Calamity said later that she rounded up his killer with a meat cleaver and helped hang him, but that was just another of her tall tales.

Fraternity Hall, Elkhorn, ghost town

In her later years, Calamity was often arrested for disorderly conduct; she might suddenly be taken with the idea of shooting at strangers' feet or perforating saloon floors with bullets. In one Montana town, she led an uproarious bunch of cowboys in a wild ride down the street, all of them yelling and shooting.

In 1902, the year before she died, she took after a store clerk in Billings with an ax and landed in jail—not for the first time, by any means.

Calamity Jane died just one day before the twenty-seventh anniversary of Wild Bill Hickok's death, and her last words were, "Bury me by Bill." So they did. The graves are side by side in Deadwood, South Dakota.

Gary Cooper

Montana is very proud of a Helena boy, Frank Cooper, son of the late Charles H. Cooper, associate justice of the State Supreme Court. Frank was born in Helena in 1901, went to school in England and to college in Grinnell, Iowa, and aspired to be a cartoonist. But he became an outstanding movie star with his first name changed: Gary Cooper.

Although Gary Cooper made dozens of Western movies, he didn't play Western heroes exclusively. He starred in two of Ernest Hemingway's stories, *Farewell to Arms* and *For Whom the Bell Tolls*, and became a close friend of that author. He won an Academy Award in *Sergeant York*, a war picture, and another for *High Noon*. The list of his starring roles went on and on.

Gary Cooper died in 1961. One of his last roles was as Doc Frail in *The Hanging Tree*, a Western about a gold camp. I had a special interest in that movie because I wrote the book.

I met My Hero when he came to Missoula with the producers and his stand-in. They were looking for a location to make the picture. They took me to dinner. (I was too excited to eat, but I drank five cups of coffee.) With a twinkle and a smile, the great man kissed my hand. Hand kissing is something we don't go for very often in Montana, but he suspected it would please me, and it did. My story is that I didn't wash that hand for two weeks.

When the group went on to Dillon to look for a location, Gary and his stand-in, who used to live there, went into a bar where the men remembered the stand-in and greeted him enthusiastically. Pointing his thumb at the great movie star, he remarked, "I suppose you recognize this fellow?"

And none of them did! When he was identified, everybody, including Gary Cooper, had a good laugh. This is the kind of cut-'em-down-to-size story that Montana people love, even though our Gary Cooper never needed cutting down to size because he never put on airs.

Granville Stuart

Granville Stuart was the very prototype of Western pioneers. With his brother, James, he came to Montana when its only non-Indian inhabitants were a handful of missionaries and a few adventurers. James died young; Granville lived, in spite of the perils he passed through, to the age of eighty-four.

During his long lifetime, he traded with the Indians, prospected for gold, ran a general store, raised cattle, executed rustlers, and served his country as a diplomat in South America. He was a man of infinite variety.

Granville attended country school as a boy for only a few short terms in Iowa, but he had the inclination of a scholar and through his own efforts he became an educated man. Once when he and James, then living in frontier Montana, heard from an Indian that another man had some books, the brothers saddled up and rode 150 miles, crossing three rivers at flood stage. They bought five books at $5 apiece—spending half the money they possessed. When Granville was an old man, he still had those books.

In the spring of 1862, Granville married a Snake Indian girl named Aubony. He cherished her until her death twenty-five years later, unlike many other pioneers who took Indian wives and treated them badly. Granville and Aubony had nine children.

Granville believed in education, and before there were public schools, he always had a teacher at the ranch for his children. His second wife, Miss Isabel Allis Brown, had been one of these teachers.

Granville and James hunted for gold and found it—but they didn't profit much. They were part owners of a general store in Virginia City during the dangerous days of the road agents. Twenty years later, Granville was one of the cattle kings of Montana, part owner of vast herds that roamed on the open range. When he was an old man, he wrote that in 1883 the fall roundup showed that 3 percent

109

of his cattle had been lost by thievery. In his dry, witty way, he said:

"Near our home ranch we discovered one rancher whose cows invariably had twin calves and frequently triplets, while the range cows in that vicinity were nearly all barren and would persist in hanging around this man's corral, envying his cows their numerous children and bawling and lamenting their own childless fate. This state of affairs continued until we were obliged to call around that way and threaten to hang the man if his cows had any more twins."

This was no idle threat. Granville organized a vigilance committee of fourteen stockmen to deal with organized bands of rustlers. He never divulged the names of the men who rode with him. When an angry woman accused him of hanging thirty innocent men, he raised his hat and replied politely, "Yes, madam, and I did it alone."

This vigilance committee became known both as Stuart's Stranglers and as the Montana Assassination—neither name intended as complimentary. In one raid, nine stock growers led by Granville attacked eleven horse thieves and killed six of them in a gunfight. Four got away but were captured by a law officer and hanged by a masked posse that took them away from him. One of the rustlers was Granville's own nephew. The vigilantes rounded up 284 stolen horses and had very little trouble after that.

The Terrible Winter of 1886–87 ruined Stuart's cattle empire. The thought of those tormented cattle, starving on the prairie, sickened him, and he decided that he would never again own an animal that he couldn't feed and shelter.

In 1894, Granville Stuart was appointed to a diplomatic post in Uruguay and Paraguay with the resounding title of envoy extraordinary and minister plenipotentiary. He couldn't get ship passage direct to South America, so he went by way of Europe. He lived and traveled in South America for five years.

Stuart was one of the founders of the Montana Historical Society, in 1865, and its first secretary. He was also one of the founders of the Society of Montana Pioneers and became its president. He was the first president of the territorial stock growers association.

He was commissioned by the state to write a history of Montana and was at work on it when he died in 1918.

AITING FOR A CHINOOK

The last of 5000

Russell's "Waiting for a Chinook—The Last of 5,000"

E. C. Abbott, known as Teddy Blue, was a cowboy who married Granville's daughter Mary. He was so much in love with her, he said, that when he tried to read the brand on a cow, all he could see was the name Mary.

Teddy Blue once said, "Granville Stuart lived on the frontier and he did what the frontier required of him. But he was a citizen for any state to be proud of."

He said, too, "Granville Stuart *was* the history of Montana."

Once I had the privilege of meeting Mary Stuart Abbott. Very old then, she had the dignity and the profile of an Egyptian queen, and she was as much fun to talk to as your best friend.

I realized with delight: *Why, I am talking to History's daughter!*

111

Chapter 8

What We're Like in Montana

What are the people of Montana like? We tend to be independent and don't want to be regulated more than is absolutely necessary. Once I spent a week at a vacation camp on the East Coast where we were kept busy every minute with organized fun. All the other young women liked this very well; not a minute of precious vacation time was wasted in wondering what to do next.

But I missed Montana freedom. When the lifeguard announced that we were allowed to swim only the crawl stroke, I gave up and left the place. I'm a competent swimmer, but nobody is going to lay down the law about *how* I do it. In Montana we prefer to do things our own way.

We like informality and friendliness. The better known a person is, the more likely we are to call him by his first name even if we're meeting him for the first time. Former Governor Tim Babcock once

Tobacco Root Mountains

Bitterroot National Forest

remarked that if a stranger doesn't call him Tim, he is pretty sure that man doesn't like him. When we speak or write to Montana's Senator Mike Mansfield, we call him Mike. A. B. Guthrie, Jr., famous author of *The Big Sky* and other outstanding novels, is called Bud by people who have never met him.

We consider it simply courtesy to smile at strangers we encounter. Visitors from out of the state are sometimes surprised (and usually pleased) when a gas station attendant or a waitress in a café asks, "And how are *you* today?" That's just good manners in these parts, partner. In a state with so few people in it, we care how everybody is today.

MONTANA PROFILE

The Treasure State
Land of Shining Mountains

GENERAL

Statehood   November 8, 1889; forty-first state to join the Union

Area   147,138 square miles; fourth-ranking state

Population   682,133 (1970 preliminary census); forty-second ranking state

Capital   Helena

Motto   "Oro y Plata" (Gold and Silver)

Flower   Bitterroot

Bird   Western meadowlark

Tree   Ponderosa pine

PHYSICAL CHARACTERISTICS

Boundaries

North   Canadian provinces of Saskatchewan, Alberta, and British Columbia

East   North and South Dakota

South   Wyoming

West   Idaho

Greatest width   550 miles east to west

Greatest length   318 miles north to south

Highest point   Granite Peak, 12,850 feet

Lowest point   1,800 feet above sea level (in northwestern Montana where the Kootenai River leaves the state)

Climate

Average winter temperature in east is 14°, in west, 20°; summer temperature 64° in west, 71° in east; highest recorded temperature: 117°; lowest recorded temperature: —70°; average annual precipitation 13–14 inches.

Principal cities (1970 preliminary census figures)

Billings: 60,549
Sugar and oil refineries, livestock, alfalfa, flour, vegetables, dairy and meat products, electrical equipment

Great Falls: 58,761
Hydroelectric power plants, copper and zinc reduction plants, wire mills, flour mills, livestock, dairy products, bricks, fur, beverages, communications center

Missoula: 29,232
Dairy products, grain, cattle, beet sugar, lumber, copper and lead mining

Butte: 23,171
Zinc, silver, manganese, gold, lead, arsenic, copper mining

Helena: 22,557
Cotton shipping, lumber, oil, flour, grain, potatoes, gold mining, bricks and tiles, concrete products

Bozeman: 18,138
Farming, cattle, tourist center

Havre: 10,381
Cattle, sheep, wheat, dairy products, potatoes, beverages, gas wells

Kalispell: 10,370
Fruit, flour, cereal, peas, grain, timber, silver and lead mining, tourist and trade center

Anaconda: 9,624
Mining foundries, bricks, metal castings, livestock, dairy products, beverages, potatoes

Principal lakes, natural

Big	McDonald	Salmon
Flathead	Medicine	Seeley
Kintla	Placid	Swan
Mary Ronan	St. Mary	Whitefish

Principal lakes, man-made

Fort Peck	Hauser	Holter	Hungry Horse

Principal reservoirs

Canyon Ferry	Libby	Yellowtail
Fresno	Tiber	

Principal rivers

Bitterroot	Marias	Sun
Blackfoot	Milk	Teton
Clarks Fork	Missouri	Tongue
Columbia	Powder	Yellowstone
Kootenai		

Principal mountains

Granite Peak (12,850)	Silver Run Peak (12,610)
Mount Wood (12,661)	Mount Rearguard (12,350)

LEADING PRODUCTS

(Manufactured goods, agricultural products, and minerals are listed in order of importance)

Manufacturing

Lumber, metal and petroleum products; dairy, flour, wheat products; sugar

Agriculture

Grain, cattle, sheep, sugar beets; dairy products

Minerals

Copper, fluorspar, manganese, vermiculite, petroleum, coal, lead, gold, phosphate rock, rare earth metals, zinc, natural gas, sand, gravel, silver

Tourism

Income from tourism estimated at $127,000,000. Hunting, fishing, dude ranching attract many tourists. Glacier National Park and Flathead Lake are popular recreational areas. Historic sites, such as Custer Battlefield National Cemetery in Big Horn County, attract many outside visitors.

GOVERNMENT

U.S. Congress	*State Legislature*
Senators: 2	Senators: 55
Representatives: 2	Representatives: 104
	Counties: 56
	Electoral votes: 4

Universities and Colleges (partial list)

Carroll College	Montana State University
College of Great Falls	Northern Montana College
Eastern Montana College	Rocky Mountain College
Montana College of Mineral Science and	University of Montana
Technology	Western Montana College

HISTORY

1743   The La Verendrye brothers, first white men to set foot in Montana, sight the Big Horn Mountains.

1803   Eastern Montana becomes a U.S. Territory through the Louisiana Purchase.

1805   Lewis and Clark cross Montana, westward bound.

1807   Manuel Lisa builds the first fur-trading post.

1808   David Thompson brings British fur interests from the Northwest.

1823   Jones-Immel party of fur traders attacked by Indians on the Yellowstone River.

1831   Flathead and Nez Percé Indians invite missionaries to Montana.

1841   Father De Smet establishes St. Mary's Mission at Stevensville.

1846   Northwestern Montana becomes part of the United States through the Oregon Treaty with England.

118

1847   Fort Benton established on the Missouri River.

1854   Catholic mission established at St. Ignatius.

1858   Gold discovered at Gold Creek by James and Granville Stuart.

1860   First steamboat reaches Fort Benton.

1862   Mullan Wagon Road completed between Fort Benton and Walla Walla, Washington. Gold rush to Grasshopper Creek (Bannack). James Fisk opens a route from Minnesota to the Montana goldfields.

1863   Gold rush to Alder Gulch (Virginia City).

1864   Montana Territory created. Gold rush to Last Chance Gulch (Helena). Gang of road agents broken up by vigilantes. First newspaper, *Montana Post*, published in Virginia City. First territorial legislature meets. President Andrew Johnson appoints Sidney Edgerton first governor.

1875   Territorial capital moved from Virginia City to Helena.

1876   Sioux and Cheyenne Indians wipe out the command of General George Armstrong Custer at the Little Big Horn.

1877   New forts built. Big Hole Battle; Nez Percé Indians surrender in the Bear Paw Mountains.

1880   First railroad, Utah Northern, comes into Montana from the south.

1881   Northern Pacific Railroad reaches Miles City from the east.

1884   Cattlemen form a vigilante association to fight off rustlers.

1889   Montana joins the Union as forty-first state.

1894   Helena becomes the permanent state capital.

1910   Glacier National Park established.

1911   Influx of homesteaders begins.

1912–   County splitting results in the formation of twenty-five new counties.
1920

1914   Women gain the right to vote.

1916   Jeannette Rankin becomes the first woman elected to Congress.

1924   Senator Thomas J. Walsh exposes the Teapot Dome scandal.

1951   Oil boom begins in eastern Montana.

1959   Earthquake kills twenty-eight people, dams the Madison River, and creates a new lake.

1961   Drought and grasshoppers ruin grain crop.

1964   The state's worst flood drowns thirty-four persons; damage amounts to $62,000,000.

1965   Construction of Yellowtail Dam completed.

1967   Long strike of copper miners' union begins in July.

STATE GOVERNORS

Joseph K. Toole	Democrat	1889–1893
John E. Rickards	Republican	1893–1897
Robert Burns Smith	Democrat	1897–1901
Joseph K. Toole	Democrat	1901–1908
Edwin L. Norris	Democrat	1908–1913
Sam V. Stewart	Democrat	1913–1921
Joseph M. Dixon	Republican	1921–1925
John E. Erickson	Democrat	1925–1933
Frank H. Cooney	Democrat	1933–1935
W. Elmer Holt	Democrat	1935–1937
Roy E. Ayers	Democrat	1937–1941
Sam C. Ford	Republican	1941–1949
John W. Bonner	Democrat	1949–1953
J. Hugo Aronson	Republican	1953–1961
Donald G. Nutter	Republican	1961–1962
Tim M. Babcock	Republican	1962–1969
Forrest H. Anderson	Democrat	1969–

PEOPLE AND MONTANA

The list does not necessarily include people identified in the book. You can find them in the Index.

J. Hugo Aronson (1891–   ), "The Galloping Swede," immigrant rancher, oilman, state legislator, governor.

I. G. Baker (1819–1904), trader, steamboat owner (he and T. C. Power known as "the merchant princes of the plains").

John Beidler (1831–1890), known as X, the vigilantes' hangman, law officer.

Charles Bovey (1907–   ), wheat rancher, state legislator, restored Virginia City and Nevada City as tourist attractions.

William A. Clark (1839–1925), copper-mining tycoon, financier.

R. A. Cooley (1873–1968), physician, pioneered in the study of Rocky Mountain spotted fever.

Plenty Coups (1848–1932), distinguished Crow Indian chief, friend of whites.

Marcus Daly (1841–1900), Irish immigrant, copper tycoon, famous racehorse owner.

Thomas Dimsdale (1831–1866), English-born author of *Vigilantes of Montana*, first book published in the territory.

Chet Huntley (1911–   ), Montana-born television news broadcaster.

Harvey Logan (1867–1904), alias Kid Curry, notorious outlaw.

John Owen (1818–1859), "Major," trader with the Indians at Fort Owen.

T. C. Power (1839–1923), trader, merchant, one of first Senators from state.

Jeannette Rankin (1880–   ), first woman elected to Congress in 1916, reelected in 1940.

Father Antonio Ravalli (1811–1884), Italian-born Catholic missionary to the Indians.

Wilbur Fisk Sanders (1834–1905), vigilante, lawyer, one of first Senators from state.

Bob Scriver (1914–   ), wildlife sculptor.

John Tatsey (1894–   ), Blackfoot Indian nationally known for frank and funny newspaper reporting.

William Wesley Van Orsdel (1848–1919), "Brother Van," Methodist circuit rider.

T. F. Walsh (1859–1933), U.S. Senator 1913–1933, exposed the Teapot Dome oil scandal in 1923.

PRONUNCIATION GUIDE

Butte	byoot
Cheyenne	shy *en*
Chinook	shin *ook*
Choteau	*sho* toe
Havre	*hav* ur
Helena	*hel* uh nuh
Kalispell	kal is *pel*
Makoshika	mak *osh* ik uh
Meagher	mar
Missoula	miz *oo* luh
Moiese	mo *ees*
Nez Percé	nay pair *say* (commonly, *nez* purse)
placer	*pla* sur
Ronan	ro *nan*
Sacajawea	*sac* a jah *we* ah
Teton	*tee* ton
Wibaux	*we* boe

INDEX

About the Author

Dorothy M. Johnson has spent most of her life in the state of Montana. A graduate of the University of Montana, Miss Johnson spent several years as a magazine editor in New York, then returned to teach in the University of Montana's School of Journalism. During the fourteen years of her teaching career, Miss Johnson was an active member of the Montana Press Association.

In addition to teaching journalism, Miss Johnson is the author of numerous short stories, articles, and books, including titles for young readers. Her two principal areas of interest are as diverse as they are exciting—the American West and ancient Greece. She has traveled to Greece several times and has not only made her home in the West, but is an adopted member of the Blackfoot Indian tribe! Dorothy Johnson's *The Hanging Tree* was made into a film starring Gary Cooper. Television programs and other films, including *A Man Called Horse*, have been made from her short stories.

A   D   A

SASKATCHEWAN

River

BLAINE

PHILLIPS

VALLEY

DANIELS   SHERIDAN

ROOSEVELT

Missouri   R.

Fort Peck
Reservoir

MC CONE

RICHLAND

Missouri

River

FERGUS

PETRO-
LEUM

GARFIELD

DAWSON

WIBAUX

NORTH DAKOTA

PRAIRIE

MUSSELSHELL

GOLDEN
VALLEY

TREASURE

ROSEBUD

Yellowstone   R.

CUSTER

FALLON

YELLOWSTONE

STILL-
WATER

BILLINGS

BIG HORN

POWDER
RIVER

CARTER

CARBON

WYOMING

SOUTH DAKOTA

MONTANA'S COUNTIES

50 Miles

STATES OF THE NATION

These books provide young people with a contemporary survey of the economic life, character, and resources of each of the states of the Union. They include salient events in the state's history, as well as the important facts about its geography, mineral wealth, peoples, parks, and recreational facilities. Each contains an extensive reference section which features a chronology of important moments in state history, a pronunciation guide to place-names, and a comprehensive index. And each is written in a narrative style which children will enjoy.

ALASKA
by Elsa Pedersen

ARIZONA
by Betty Baker

FLORIDA
by Mike Smith

INDIANA
by Jeannette C. Nolan

MASSACHUSETTS
by Margaret Coit

MICHIGAN
by Russel B. Nye

MONTANA
by Dorothy M. Johnson

NEVADA
by Robert Laxalt

NEW HAMPSHIRE
by Elizabeth Yates

NEW JERSEY
by Keith Robertson

NEW MEXICO
by Jack Schaefer

NORTH CAROLINA
by Thelma and Corydon Bell

OHIO
by Marion Renick

OREGON
by Iris Noble

RHODE ISLAND
by Scott Corbett

SOUTH CAROLINA
by Sally Edwards

SOUTH DAKOTA
by Nancy Veglahn

TENNESSEE
by William O. and
Allerton W. Steele

VIRGINIA
by Michael Frome

WASHINGTON
by Angelo M. Pellegrini

WEST VIRGINIA
by Felix Sutton

WISCONSIN
by August Derleth

M